Cubesat Constellations, Clusters, & Swarms

Patrick H. Stakem

Jan, 2017,
updated September, 2022.

Number 4 in the Cubesat Series

There is Strength in Numbers.

Introduction

This book discusses the application of Cubesat Clusters, Constellations, and Swarms in the exploration of the solar systems. This includes the Sun, the 8 primary planets and Pluto, numerous moons, the asteroid belt, comets, the ring systems of the four gas giants, and comets. There is a lot to explore. U.S. Spacecraft have been to all of the planets in the solar system. Although the planets (and Pluto) have been visited by spacecraft, Earth's moon has been somewhat explored, and many of the other planets' moons have been imaged, there is a lot of "filling in the blanks" to be done. Here we explore the application of groups of small independent spacecraft to take on this role. Some of the enabling technology for cooperating swarms is examined.

Missions to Mars and beyond are lengthy and expensive. We need to ensure that we are delivering payloads that will function for a while and return new data. The trade-off is between one or two large traditional spacecraft, and a new concept, a large number of nearly identical small spacecraft, operating cooperatively. Necessarily, the Technology Readiness Level of this approach must be proven in Earth orbit, before the resources are allocated to extend this approach to distant locations. Decades of time, and hundreds of millions of dollars are at stake.

The big picture is, Cubesats are not just secondary payloads anymore. They may be small, but a group of them together can accomplish a lot. We'll discuss the technologies to make this happen.

Just after this book was published, an event occurred requiring an update. Such is the march of technology. The Indian Space Research Organization (ISRO) launched 104 Cubesats from their Sriharikota launch site into Polar orbit. This was a new record for the number of satellites to orbit in one mission. It also validated the concept of Cubesats as a primary payload. They were deployed in 18 minutes. See,

https://www.nytimes.com/2017/02/15/world/asia/india-satellites-rocket.html?_r=0

88 of these were 3U "Doves" from Planet Labs of San Francisco, on an Earth Imaging mission. These carry a 90mm aperture optical payload with RGB imaging, giving a ground resolution of 3 to 5 meters. Their projected orbital lifetime, is 3 years. They use a high speed X-band downlink, with a UHF backup. The Flock, as they refer to them, can image the entire Earth every day. Effectively, they form a line scanner in the same orbit.

The Orion Stage Adapter of the upcoming mission to the Moon was built by MSFC, and can hold up to 17 tag-along Cubesats. Ten are going on the first flight. By weight, Artemis could carry 27,900 Cubesats, but probably doesn't have enough space.

The Author

Mr. Stakem has been interested in rockets and spacecraft since high school. He received a Bachelor's degree in Electrical Engineering from Carnegie-Mellon University in 1971, where he was a member of the Applied Space Sciences group. His first job was for Fairchild Industries, then building the ATS-6 spacecraft. Wernher von Braun joined Fairchild as Vice-President of Engineering during this time, so, technically, Mr. Stakem was once a member of the von Braun Team. Specializing in support of spacecraft onboard computers, he has worked at every NASA Center. He supported the Apollo-Soyuz mission with the ATS-6 communications satellite. He received Master's degrees in Physics and Computer Science from the Johns Hopkins University. He has taught for Loyola University in Maryland, Graduate Department of Computer Science, AIAA, The Johns Hopkins University, Whiting School of Engineering, and Capitol Technology University.

He served for several years as a Mentor for NASA, Goddard Space Flight Center's Engineering bootcamp, which brought together international teams of students to work on real projects. This resulted in the deployment of the Grover (Greenland Rover), a large "satellite" operating at zero altitude. It collects data on the thickness of the Greenland Ice Sheet.

He has also been active in the summer Cubesat program at Capitol Technology University, teaching classes and mentoring student projects. He may be found on

Facebook and Linkedin.

This book is number 3 in the Cubesat Series, initially published in the first quarter of 2017. The series includes Cubesat Engineering, Cubesat Operations, Cubesat Constellations, Clusters, and Swarms, and Interplanetary Cubesats.

Cubesats

A Cubesat is a small, affordable satellite that can be developed and launched by college, high schools, and even individuals. The specifications were developed by Academia in 1999. Cubesats are built to a standard architecture. The basic structure is a 10 centimeter cube, (volume of 1 liter) weighing less than 1.33 kilograms. This allows several of these standardized packages to be launched as secondary payloads on other missions Standard cubesat dispensers have been developed, the Poly-PicoSat Orbital Deployer, P-POD, that holds multiple Cubesats and dispenses them on orbit is one. They can also be deployed from the Space Station, via a custom airlock. ESA, the United States, Russia, and numerous commercial outfits provide launch services. The Cubesat origin lies with Prof. Twiggs of Stanford University and was proposed as a vehicle to support hands-on university-level space education and opportunities for low-cost space access.

In what has been called the Revolution of smallsats, Cubesats lead the way. They represent paradigm shifts in developing space missions, opening the field from National efforts and large Aerospace contractors, to individuals and schools.

Even though individuals have built, launched, and operated Cubesats, the application of more than one is beyond a single individuals' capabilities, and budget, at the moment.

Central to the Cubesat concept is the standardization of the interface between the launch vehicle and the spacecraft, which allows developers to pool together for launch and so reduce costs and increase opportunities. As a university-led initiative, Cubesat developers have advocated many cost-saving mechanisms, namely:

- A reduction in project management and quality assurance roles .

- Use of student labor with expert oversight to design, build and test key subsystems.

- Reliance on non-space-rated Commercial-Off-The-Shelf (COTS) components .

- Limited or no built-in redundancy (compensated for by the parallel development of multiple Cubesats) .

- Access to launch opportunities through standardized launch interfaces.

- Use of amateur communication frequency bands and support from amateur ground stations.

- Simplicity in design, architecture and objective.

This approach has since been adopted by numerous universities and organizations around the globe, and to date has been used as the basis of 40 missions (at the end of October 2008) with many active projects in development. High schools and individuals are also pursuing Cubesat projects. The launch cost is a major issue, but multiple Cubesats can be carried as secondary payloads on military and commercial flights. You don't always get your choice of orbit, but you can get close. This is referred to as ride sharing. Its like hitch-hiking.

Since the initial proposal of the concept, continuing efforts have been made to define internal and external interfaces by various developers of Cubesat subsystems, products and services that have defined the Cubesat 'standard' as it is today. A core strength of the Cubesat is its recognition of the need for flexibility in the definition of standards, and since conception the standard has evolved to ensure that these design rules are as open as possible. The most significant of these further advances in definition have been for the POD deployment systems (in order to meet launch requirements) and the modularization of the internal electronics.

The in-orbit success rate of university-led Cubesat projects (not withstanding launch failures) is around 50%; this is an understandable result of using the Cubesat as an education tool. Development itself is a learning process and in-orbit failure is a disappointment but should not be considered the primary focus. For projects involving significant participation of companies with experience in satellite development, all but one were a success and demonstrated the strength of the Cubesat for non-educational applications. It is estimated that at least

12 Cubesat missions could be considered to have demonstrated significant successful in-orbit operations for a sustained period. All Cubesats missions to date may be considered to have had technological objectives to some degree, be it the demonstration of devices and system architectures developed in-house, or demonstration of Non-Space-Rated (NSR) Commercial-Off-The-Shelf (COTS) component performance. Some Cubesats have also attempted to fulfill other mission objectives, although categorizing these accurately can be difficult

A simple Cubesat controller can be developed from a standard embedded computing platform such as the Arduino or Raspberry Pi. The lack of radiation hardness can be balanced by the short on-orbit lifetime. The main drivers for a Cubesat flight computer are small size, small power consumption, wide functionality, and flexibility. In addition, a wide temperature range is desirable. The architecture supports a real time operating system, but, in the simplest case, a simple loop program with interrupt support can work.

Earth imaging is a common objective for a Cubesat mission, typically achieved using a CMOS camera without any complex lens systems. As a critical impediment to the development of a highly capable platform for mission operations, the testing and evaluation of novel approaches for increasing downlink data rate and reliability is also a common objective. While less common than Earth imaging, real science objectives are becoming increasingly popular as recognition (primarily by NASA) of Cubesat capabilities increase and collaborations between engineering and science groups emerge.

Additional capabilities of proposed future missions either in planning or in development include: space weather monitoring, inflatable de-orbit devices, Earth imaging with optical lens, cosmic ray showers, shape memory alloys, star mapping, data relay, re-programmable computing, nano-meteorid dust, plasma probe, and multi-spectral remote sensing.

Cost reduction in these projects has been achieved through a number of mechanisms, some of which are unavailable to the conventional space industry. The lowest cost yet successful mission is reported to be estimated as under $100,000 (although that mission was not fitted with solar arrays). A typical cost for a university project varies considerably but a very approximate estimation might be from $50,000 to $150,000 for launch and $5-$10,000. in parts cost per unit. Piggyback launches have been offered for free to Cubesats by launch vehicle operators and space agencies, negating the majority of launch cost.

Another important and related aspect in the design approach is that of modularity in a complete and integrated Cubesat life cycle, effectively representing a modular system of systems. The accelerated life cycle demonstrated consistently by small satellites, and harnessed by many Cubesat developers, can be further enhanced by the application of modularity to the complete life cycle. Cubesats are ideal teaching tools for aerospace engineering students, even if they are not going to fly. The same extends down into High School, and Grade School.

Cubesats can fly alone, as secondary payloads with other missions, such as the MARCO Project to Mars, and in Swarms. The MARCO mission has 2 Cubesat fly-alongs, that separate after launch, and continue to Mars along with the primary payload.

NASA Involvement with Cubesats

NASA has been exploring the usage of "Smallsats" for some time, to reduce mission costs and provide rapid development and deployment. When Cubesats came along from the University environment, it didn't take long for NASA to embrace the technology.

NASA GSFC says, "Current technology trends indicate a shift in satellite architectures from large, single-satellite missions to small, distributed spacecraft missions. At the center of this shift is the SmallSat/CubeSat architecture."

At NASA and many National Labs, Cubesats have been a game-changer. The cost to develop, build, and test a concept or technology has gone down by orders of magnitude. This precursor technology has not only gone down in price, but the implementation process has been accelerated.

A NASA/GSFC Cubesat project, Dellingr, is in orbit It is 6U (12" x 8" x 4") size. It was a three-year project to design, develop, test, and integrate the unit. It went to the International Space Station. It is a Heliophysics payload, carrying an ion/neutral mass spectrometer. The design was made available as Open Source after the mission was kicked off.

Another project was the NSF-funded Firefly mission, launched in November of 2013, and now returning good data on terrestrial Gamma ray flashes, These are interesting phenomena, involving high energy electrons generated by thunderstorms. Firefly uses a Pumpkin flight motherboard for avionics, based on the Texas Instruments MSP430 chip. That unit is a 16-bit RISC micro-controller architecture, The unit is ultra-low power, and mixed signal, supporting analog. It includes a real-time clock, and non-volatile FRAM memory.

Cubesats provide a relatively low cost alternative for proof of concept, and TRL advancement (explained below). We're talking $1 million, not $100 million. We take advantage of the modularity and standardization of open source hardware and software. We have, essentially, *Plug-and-play* satellite buses, provided by an evolving infrastructure of parts suppliers.

Generally, Cubesats are not allowed to have a propulsion system. They are specifically constrained to not exhaust any gas, even nitrogen. However, NASA can use propulsion on their own small satellites. Another way for Cubesats to wander the solar system is via solar sails, which use the solar wind, emanating from the Sun, much as a sailboat uses the terrestrial wind. Currently, the CubeSat mission to Mars, MARCO, uses tag-along Cubesats, launched with the primary payload, and proceeding along their own path.

13

More than one

Here we discuss aggregations of Cubesats. They may interact with each other. Some of the architectures include Trains, Constellations, Clusters, and Swarms. These techniques have been used with conventional spacecraft for years. An interesting point is, not all the members of the groups need to be launched or deployed at the same time. Beyond deploying Cubesats as ride-along payloads, we can postulate a very large Cubesat carrier with hundreds or thousands of Units, being delivered to a target of interest. The Cubesats here are the primary payload. The Constellations can be "grown" and expand as the mission progresses, and failed units can be replaced.

The Virginia Cubesat Constellation was a colloboration of the Virginia Space Grant Consortium, Old Dominion University, Virginia Tech, University of Virginia, asnd Hampton University. There were three nano-sats, built to study the Earth's atmosphere. The Cubesat were first sent brought up to the ISS, and then deployed through Nanaracks Cubesat deployer.

Trains

Trains of satellites refer to multiple units that are spaced along the same orbital track. This allows for simultaneous imaging areas, as well as continuous observation of selected areas. It is a co-ordinated group of observation satellites. NASA uses this approach successfully for Earth Science and Weather satellites in polar, sun-synchronous orbits. A train of 6 weather satellites passes over the same spot at the same time every day. The satellites are all different, but provide useful information on atmospheric and ground conditions. Another term for a simple group of spacecraft in the same orbit is *string-of-pearls*.

A single orbit with four sun-synchronous Disaster Monitoring Constellation (DMC) satellites was implemented in 2002-2003. A second Constellation was implemented with 4 additional satellites by 2011. with participation by the U.K., Algeria, Nigeria, Turkey, and China.

Clusters

In computing, a cluster means a group of loosely coupled compute elements, working together on the same problem. If the cluster were more tightly coupled, and self-directed, we'd have a swarm. As it is, we have a group of individuals that could be considered a single entity. Generally, members of a compute cluster have the same hardware and software configuration. One issue in clustering is the degree of coupling between elements. No coupling means we have a mob. A lot of coupling and we might have a swarm. In a cluster, management of the cluster itself can be centralized in a control unit, or can be distributed across the cluster. An example computer cluster is the NASA-developed Beowulf architecture, applicable to Raspberry Pi hosts.

Constellations

Constellations are groups of satellites operating together

to observe a single target A constellation allows you to do simultaneous observations of one target from multiple locations, or multiple targets simultaneously. The elements of a constellation can be homogeneous or not.

NASA says, " A Constellation is a space mission that, beginning with its inception, is composed of two or more spacecraft that are placed into specific orbit(s) for the purpose of serving a common objective (e.g., Iridium)." (The Iridium constellation is for communications).

Other examples include the Galileo Constellation of European navigation satellites, the US GPS navigation satellites, and NASA's Tracking & Data Relay Satellites, at Geosynchronous orbit. Internet via satellite link is provided to the scientific community in Antarctica by a constellation of polar orbiting comm-sats.

An actual "constellation" of 50 2U and 3U Cubesats was deployed in 2015. Some were released from the ISS, and some from a rocket launch. They collected and telemetered data on the lower thermospere. This is not true Constellation, but 50 units acting on their own, reporting back to their home institutions. Universities around the world participated, and built units from the QB50 specification.

The Distributed Spacecraft Mission was defined at JPL to allow "formation flying" of multiple spacecraft. Another point of view is the "fractionalized spacecraft", where the spacecraft functionality is distributed across multiple units. Critical to this is a intra-communications mechanism. The Constellation may use a mesh or lattice architecture. The members of this organization can be launched together, or separately. One thing for sure, each unit needs a unique identifier.

Constellations of Cubesat have found a niche in looking down to see the health of crops in the field. This technique has been used for quite a while, using large satellites. Goddard Space Flight Center is located in a repurposed area of the Nationasl Agriculture Farm. This is administered by the Department of Agriculture, and include both animals and crops. In calibrating the Landsat imagers, they would compare the data with what they saw locally, a technique called ground truth.

A Mesh network is highly interconnected. We may emulate this with a Mesh of Cubesats, each with communication with all the other units. In Mesh computer networking, each node relays data between units. That's pretty much how the Internet works, with store-and-forward nodes. Most Mesh networks use a routing protocol. A fully connected network has all nodes connected to each other. This works for a small number of nodes, but gets overly complex as the network grows. IEEE 802.11s is an IEEE standard for wireless mesh networking. You may be using this standard right at this moment. Mesh network topologies are well understood.

Ad-hoc networks, such as used in cellular communications work well on Earth, but in space, we may have long distances to communicate with significant delays, This is addressed in mobile data networks, called mobile ad-hoc networks (MANET).

Several approaches to communication with spacecraft at large distances from Earth, and examining other planets, have been defined. The Interplanetary Internet implements a Bundle Protocol to address large and variable delays. Normal IP traffic assumes a seamless, end-to-end, available data path, without worrying about the physical mechanism. The Bundle protocol addresses the cases of high probability of errors, and disconnections. This protocol was tested in communication with an Earth orbiting satellite in 2008.

These units can be statically or dynamically allocated. We might have a fixed plan for location and function, or it might be ad hoc, responding to conditions as they are encountered.

For Cubesats, we need a "mothership" that takes the Cubesats to their destination, then sticks around to manage and support. This approach will be discussed in a section on the Pinesat multi-Cubesat mission to Jupiter, later in the book.

Complexity in a system generally derives from two parameters, the number of units, and the number of interactions. So a swarm of cubesats could be said to be complex, compared to a single spacecraft. This is somewhat balanced by the relative simplicity of the units, and their flexibility and redundancy.

Constellation missions are difficult to design, because of their uniqueness and complexity. The parameters are necessarily mission-dependent. For homogeneous constellations in the same orbit, the Walker-Delta design, developed in 1970, is often used. A more recent concept , the Flower Constellation, from Texas A&M university is being used. I will not get into the orbital design here, due to its complexity. Rest assured, for any mission, the tools exist to design the orbital geometry. Actually, that's not quite right. At the moment we have no known solution to put a probe out of the plane of the ecliptic to view the solar poles. A few Cubesats would be a good choice for that mission.

One issue for multi-spacecraft missions in Earth Orbit is potential collisions, resulting in space debris. Although collisions between satellites have occurred, I know of none between members of a constellation.

Swarms

A driver in the space environment is the exploration of the asteroids, numbering in the thousands. Although there are fewer than 10 planets, and less than 200 moons, there are millions of asteroids, mostly in the inner solar system. The main asteroid belt is between Mars and Jupiter. Each may be unique, and some will provide needed raw materials for Earth's use. There are three main classifications: carbon-rich, stony, and metallic.

The physical composition of asteroids is varied and poorly understood. Ceres appears to be composed of a rocky core covered by an icy mantle, whereas Vesta may have a nickel-iron core. Hygiea appears to have a uniformly primitive composition of carbonaceous chondrite. Many of the smaller asteroids are piles of rubble held together loosely by gravity. Some have moons themselves, or are co-orbiting binary asteroids. The bottom line is, asteroids are numerous and diverse.

It has been suggested that asteroids might be used as a source of materials that are rare or exhausted on earth (asteroid mining) or materials for constructing space habitats or as refueling stations for missions. Materials that are heavy and expensive to launch from earth may someday be mined from asteroids and used for space manufacturing. Valuable materials such as platinum may be returned to Earth for a profit.

Exploring the asteroids requires a diverse and agile system. Thus, a swarm of robotic spacecraft with different capabilities might be used, combining into Teams of Convenience to address situations and issues discovered in situ.

Biological swarms, such as ants, achieve success by division of labor throughout the swarm, collaboration, and sheer numbers. They have redundancy, as any individual can do any task assigned to the swarm. The individual units are highly autonomous, but are dependent on other members for their needs. They achieve success with a simple neural architecture and primitive communications.

In Swarm robotics, the key issues are communication between units, and cooperative behavior. The capability of individual units nodes not much matter; it is the strength in numbers. Ants and other social insects such as termites, wasps, and bees, are models for robot swarm behavior. Self-organizing behavior emerges from decentralized systems that interact with members of the group, and the environment. Swarm intelligence is an emerging field, and swarm robotics is in its infancy. Co-operative behavior, enabled by software and intra-unit communications has been demonstrated.

A Swarm exploration of the asteroid belt was proposed by Curtis, et al, in 2003. They baselined 1,000 units. They defined 8-10 types of *Workers,* each with specific capabilities. Units assigned to swarm cohesion and communication they termed *Messengers.* There are also *Rulers*, who function in a managerial role.

They postulate target selection according to mission goals, but also mention that mission goals change as data is collected at the site. The concept of multiple spacecraft coming together to form virtual instruments is discussed. Here, we might have simultaneous observations from multiple points.

The Operational Concept involves teams that produce data and some higher level products, which are communicated to Messengers, and archived. The Rulers oversee data flow. When a sufficient amount is collected, a Messenger will be dispatched to carry it back (Today, this could be accomplished with radio or laser link).

Swarms can be implemented with central control (Master-helper) or distributed control (multi-master).

Multi-spacecraft support

The satellite control center can handle a constellation, cluster, or swarm of multiple spacecraft. Examples include the GPS constellation, the weather satellite systems, TDRSS, and a number of commercial communications satellites, providing entertainment and data service world-wide. Constellations of communication satellites are used for commercial ventures such as DishNetwork, a satellite TV provider, and Iridium and GlobalStar, communications constellations.

Managing a constellation adds to the complexity. Even if each spacecraft is built to the same plan, different spacecraft, launched at different times, and having differing times on-orbit, need customized attention. The most important aspect is to have a unique identifier, so you know which spacecraft you're talking and listening to.

An approach to Constellation control centers can involve a hierarchy of a master control center and with multiple space assets to control, or a peer network of individual control centers, that also provides a built-in redundancy and backup. A backup control center is useful not only for anomalies at the primary center, but also to allow for maintenance and upgrade of the primary center, and for personnel training and certification.

An ongoing debate in the optimum architecture for multi-satellite control is between a centralized design, and a distributed architecture. Centralized is the legacy approach. Distributed takes advantage of advances in networking and abstraction. In the distributed approach, multiple ground stations and control centers are linked by existing terrestrial data communication resources.

The distributed architecture scales more freely, with computation, storage, and communications resources being added as demand increases. High system reliability and security can be maintained from industry best practices. The scalable, distributed technology has been driven by large data-centric organizations such as Google, and retailers such as Amazon, as well as social media sites such as Facebook and Utube.

Another advantage of the distributed approach is dynamic allocation of resources, having (and paying for) resources when you need them, not all the time. The system provides mission safety simultaneously with cost effectiveness. A metric of interest is the staff to spacecraft ratio. If domain-skilled staff can be shared among the constellation, yet be brought together in the case of anomalies, personnel costs can be contained. Distributed approaches give economy of scale.

A major constellation is NOAA's Polar and Geostationary weather and environmental satellites. The USAF operates the Global Positioning System (GPS) Constellation.

The USAF maintains a world-wide satellite control network. The 2nd Space Operations Squadron in Colorado is typical of the units involved in constellation operations. The system has been in existence for decades, starting in the mainframe era of the 1970s, transitioning to the client-server architecture, and being modernized to pc and server architecture. Extensive training for operators is provided.

The same information for each spacecraft in a homogeneous constellations provides summaries of critical cross-platform information. If we just had a failure on one spacecraft, we will look for that to happen on others. A merged database, allows for trending information to flow forward. As constellations age, the individual members age and fail at different rates. From trending data on early failures, the remaining spacecraft can be monitored especially for known failures and degradation.

Several approaches will not only lower the cost of Cubesat swarm approaches, but provide additional flexibility. As an example, the COSMOS open source control center product can handle multiple spacecraft simultaneously. It depends on the capabilities of the hosting hardware as to how many spacecraft can be supported simultaneously. That depends on the cpu and memory resources of the host. It is a scalable approach.

During a recent Cubesat Operations Course, the concept of Control Center as a Service evolved. This means the control center software is hosted "in the cloud" much like Amazon or Gmail. Here, you pay for MIPS and Gbytes. The solution scales as you need it. If one node starts to get overwhelmed, you can dynamically add nodes. There is no Apollo-era Control room. Everything is on the web (with proper consideration for security, particularly for commands), and you access your Cubesat(s) from your phone or tablet, anywhere. Amazon and Google will argue that their requirements for availability and security exceed that of a space mission.

We also explored the concept of a virtual operations controller. Standard control center software can text you when a value is at its yellow or red limits. We can expand that to look at combinations of telemetry points, and also have a rule-based program to examine the status. As the program evolves, and the software gets more capable (I hesitate to say, learns), the virtual ops controller can handle more of the routine monitoring and housekeeping tasks, and some of the upfront anomaly response.

For interplanetary missions, supporting a collection of spacecraft at a distance with significant communications delay becomes more challenging. The typical delay for low Earth orbiting satellites is several milliseconds.

Tools

Various tools have been developed to simulate Constellations. The Open source SaVi satellite constellation visualizer is one (see, http://savi.sourceforge.net/). It is useful for simulating the orbits and viewing the ground coverage. AVM Dynamics has its SCModeler version 3.4, which is a modeling environment for satellite swarms.

(https://www.avmdynamics.com/software1.htm)
Simulating Satellites and Satellite Constellations using Ns2 and Other Tools, see http://www.projectguideline.com/simulating-satellites-and-satellite-constellations-using-ns2-and-other-tools/

Communications

Cubesats have a number of communications options at Earth orbit. There are several internet locations where Cubesat telemetry is posted. You can build your own receiver/transmitter, and joint a network. One of these is called, Satnogs. It uses a Yagi antenna, and a software defined radio based on the Raspberry Pi. The problem of communications and control gets tricky for multiple targets, but it depends on how many units are visible, and for how long. A train would be easy to work with. A Swarm would have a master unit that would communication with all the swarm members locally, and then aggregate the data and send it to Earth. Similarly, it would received tagged commands for swarm members, and forward those as needed.

NASA's Space Network

The Space Network (SN) dates back to the early 1980's, when NASA introduced a constellation of satellites (TDRSS) to replace the earlier STDN ground tracking stations. The TDRS network was declared operational in 1989. STDN stations at Wallops Island, Bermuda, Merritt Island (FL), Ponce de Leon (FL), and Dakar, Senegal, remained operational. The Tracking & Data Relay Satellite System is over 30 years old, and is being refreshed with new technology. The Space Segment has spare assets in orbit in case of failure. Generally, organizations and individuals can rent time on the Space Network, but it is rather pricey.

NASA's Deep Space Network

NASA's Deep Space Network consists of three antenna sites spaced around our planet. It supports deep space missions for NASA and other entities. It is managed by the Jet Propulsion Lab (JPL) in Pasadena, California. The nearest station to JPL is at Goldstone, in the desert to the east. Two other stations, in Spain and Australia are spaced about 120 degrees apart on the globe from Goldstone. The DSN started operations in the 1960's, and is heavily oversubscribed, supporting numerous deep space missions.

Several approaches to communication with spacecraft at a large distance from Earth, and examining other planets, have been defined. The Interplanetary Internet implements a Bundle Protocol to address large and variable delays. Normal IP traffic assumes a seamless, end-to-end, available data path, without worrying about the physical mechanism. The Bundle protocol addresses the cases of high probability of errors, and disconnections. This protocol was tested in communication with an Earth orbiting satellite in 2008.

As we get farther from Earth, the Cubesat's small antennas, and relatively low power, means we have to get clever with communications. There will be a limited bandwidth. This was the case with the New Horizon's spacecraft at Pluto – It took more than 16 months to transmit all the encounter data back.

In some cases, if the Earth is behind the Sun from the spacecraft's point of view, communication is not possible. Adverse space weather events also affect communications.

Group Communications

Several approaches to communication with spacecraft at a large distance from Earth, and examining other planets, have been defined. The Interplanetary Internet implements a Bundle Protocol to address large and variable delays. Normal IP traffic assumes a seamless, end-to-end, available data path, without worrying about the physical mechanism. The Bundle protocol addresses the cases of high probability of errors, and disconnections. This protocol was tested in communication with an Earth orbiting satellite in 2008.

As we get farther from Earth, the Cubesat's small antennas, and relatively low power, means we have to get clever with communications. One approach is to have the Dispenser/Mothership handle communications with Earth, and have short-range communications with the Cubesats. The Mothership may support communications between the various units as well.

Cubesat to Mothership could be UHF. It does not necessarily need to implement a delay tolerant protocol, since the Cubesats will be "in the vicinity" of the Mothership.

Electrical Power

Electrical power is a critical resource. The power system of the spacecraft will consist of batteries, solar cells for recharging, and a charge regulator. In Earth orbit, the spacecraft is constantly moving from full sun to Earth shadow each orbit. Sometimes, the available energy in the batteries must be taken into account when planning operations. Big power users are telemetry transmission, imaging, and onboard computation.

The Sun is not a good source of power for solar cells at Jupiter and beyond. Solar arrays can provide about $1/25^{th}$ of the power produced in Earth orbit, at Jupiter. It gets worse the further you are from the Sun.

The RTG for the New Horizons Pluto mission weighed in at 56 kg, and had a power availability of 300 watts at the beginning of the mission. More efficient units are being developed. A by-product of the production of power is heat, which can be handy to keep critical electronics warm enough. It can also be radiated to cold space.

A world wide shortage of plutonium fuel made the Jupiter-Juno mission use the next generation of more efficient solar cells.

Shared Databases

Each member of the Swarm will be self-documenting. It will carry a copy of its Electronic Data Sheet (EDS) description, which can be updated. This defines the system architecture and capabilities, and has both fixed (as-built) and variable (what failed) entries. The main computer in the mothership has a copy of all of these, and can get updates by query. The Mothership also has parameters on each unit's state, such as electrical power remaining, temperature, etc. One value of the database is, if the mothership needs a unit with a high resolution imager, it knows what unit that is, and whether it has been deployed or not. If it has been deployed, it can query the unit on its position and health status. Implementing the EDS in a true database has advantages, since the position of the data item in the database also carries information. It also allows use of off-the-shelf database tools. The individual CubeSats have a "light-weight" database, while the mothership has a more sophisticated one. The Motherships' own EDS is also stored in its database. All the schema's are the same.

The Mothership is responsible for aggregating all of the Cubesat's housekeeping and science data, and transmitting it back to Earth. This is also facilitated by the structure imposed by the database. An Open Source version of an SQL database is preferred. Sqlite is preferred for the Cubesats. The EDS documents could be in XML.

The Control Center's command and telemetry will also be stored in a database. If a compatible architecture is used across the flight and ground units, major operational efficiencies can be shown. The control center will also host and share the units' EDS's. You can think of incoming telemetry, or you can think of database updates.

Beginning efforts

NASA is building a "virtual telescope" using two

Cubesats. They are imaging the Sun, in a mission called "Cubesat Astronomy by NASA and Yonsei using Virtual Telescope alignment experiment," CanyVAL-X. Two spacecraft, flying in coordination and aligned with the Sun are being used. The one closest to the sun blocks the solar sphere, allowing the second spacecraft to image the outer regions of the solar atmosphere. The spacecraft are named Tom and Jerry. Jerry is smaller (1U), and Tom (2U) is between Jerry and the Sun. They both have solar sensors, Tom uses a camera to look at Jerry's laser beacons to keep alignment. The spacecraft are separated by 10 meters. This is an early proof-of-concept mission that wasaunched in 2017. The mission costs around $1 million which is a lot for 2 Cubesats, but a drop in the bucket for a full sized spacecraft. Unfortunately, in this case the spacecraft failed in space.

An overview of the Problem – Solar system exploration by Swarm's

Let's look at the number of objects in our solar system that we would like to know more about, We will also list the one way light times for the various objects. This tell us how long a radio signal takes to traverse that distance.

Trojan Asteroids – in orbit with the primary, in front and behind (4th and 5th Lagrange points).

Earth – 1 moon, 1 Trojan. Earth's moon is about ½ light second away.

NEO's - > 15,000

Technically, an NEO is a solar system object whose closest approach to the Sun is 1.3 AU, and that comes in close proximity to the Earth There are 14,000 known asteroids in this category, 100 comets, solar orbiting spacecraft, and meteoroids. All these have the potential of striking the Earth. They are closely tracked from the ground, by NASA's Planetary Defense Coordination Office. A joint US/EU project called Spaceguard is tracking NEO's larger than 30 meters. Three NEO's have been visited by spacecraft. Cubesats, with solar sails, are an ideal approach to explore objects in our home vicinity, because of the danger they may express, but also for possible exploitation by mining.

Planets

Mercury - no moons.

Venus – no moons. Has Trojans.

Asteroid belt – Ceres the dwarf planet, and 750,000 rocks
    arger than 1 km.

Mars, its 2 moons and 7 Trojans. On-way light time
    vary between 3 and 29 minutes.

Jupiter and its 80nown moons, 6,000 Trojans, 33-53
    minutes one-way light time.

Saturn and its 83moons,1.4 hours one-way light time.

Uranus and it's 27 moons, 2.7 hours one-way light time. known Trojan.

Neptune and its 14 moons, 4.3 hours one-way light time, 8 Trojans.

Pluto and its moons Charon, Nix, Hydra, Styx and Kerberos, 4.6 hours one-way light time.

Comets – 5, 253 known.

Centaurs

icy minor planets between Jupiter and Neptune, 3 known.

Kuiper Belt

The Kuiper Belt extends from the orbit of Neptune out approximately 50 AU. There are three known dwarf planets, the former planet Pluto, Ceres, Eris, Haumea, Makemake, and a bunch more. Over 100,000 are speculated to exist. It depends on the definition, which is a point of debate. Neptune has a major influence over the Kuiper belt objects. Not much is known about the belt and its objects, since astronomers have had to rely on ground based observation. The *New Horizons* mission is proceeding out through the Kuiper belt, and is reporting back what it sees. Beyond the Kuiper belt is the Scattered disc, extending beyond 100 AU. So many targets of interest, so few explorers, so little time.

I didn't total all this up, but it doesn't seem like this is a small task. We need to get a lot of spacecraft working on it. U.S. spacecraft have visited all of the planets, some of the moons, and a few of the asteroids in the Solar System (including the demoted Pluto).

First Interplanetary Cubesats

The MARCO mission, in 2018, had 2 6-U Cubesat fly alongs. They separate after launch, and continue to Mars along with the primary payload, a rover. The Cubesats serve as a real-time communications relay with Earth during the critical descent and landing phase of the rover. The Rover talks to the Cubesat relays over an 8kbps UHF link, and the Cubesats send this to Earth over an 8kbps X-band link to the DSN. The Cubesat's X-band antenna is a large flat panel. MARCO has successfully returned the its first images.

Enabling technology for the employment of Swarms of Cubesats

This section discusses the technology approaches which will enable deploying swarms of Cubesats for interplanetary exploration. This method uses a swarm of Cubesats as the primary payload. First, we have to discuss a standardized method to assess the maturity of the technology for space use.

Technology Readiness Levels

The Technology readiness level (TRL) is a measure of a facility's maturity for use. There are different TRL definitions by different agencies (NASA, DoD, ESA, FAA, DOE, etc). TRL are based on a scale from 1 to 9, with 9 being the most mature technology. The use of TRLs enables consistent, uniform, discussions of technical maturity across different types of technology. We will discuss the NASA one here, which was the original definition from the 1980's. It is generally applied to flight hardware, but can be used for the associated ground support infrastructure as well.

Technology readiness levels in the National Aeronautics and Space Administration (NASA)

1. Basic principles observed and reported
This is the lowest "level" of technology maturation. At this level, scientific research begins to be translated into applied research and development.

2. Technology concept and/or application formulated
Once basic physical principles are observed, then at the next level of maturation, practical applications of those characteristics can be 'invented' or identified. At this level, the application is still speculative: there is not experimental proof or detailed analysis to support the conjecture.

3. Analytical and experimental critical function and/or characteristic proof of concept.

At this step in the maturation process, active research and development (R&D) is initiated. This must include both analytical studies to set the technology into an appropriate context and laboratory-based studies to physically validate that the analytical predictions are correct. These studies and experiments should constitute "proof-of-concept" validation of the applications/concepts formulated at TRL 2.

4. Component and/or breadboard validation in laboratory environment.

Following successful "proof-of-concept" work, basic technological elements must be integrated to establish that the "pieces" will work together to achieve concept-enabling levels of performance for a component and/or breadboard. This validation must be devised to support the concept that was formulated earlier, and should also be consistent with the requirements of potential system applications. The validation is "low-fidelity" compared to the eventual system: it could be composed of ad hoc discrete components in a laboratory

TRL's can be applied to hardware or software, components, boxes, subsystems, or systems. Ultimately, we want the TRL level for the entire systems to be consistent with our flight requirements. Some components may have higher levels than needed.

5. Component and/or breadboard validation in relevant environment.

At this level, the fidelity of the component and/or breadboard being tested has to increase significantly. The basic technological elements must be integrated with reasonably realistic supporting elements so that the total applications (component-level, sub-system level, or system-level) can be tested in a 'simulated' or somewhat realistic environment.

6. System/subsystem model or prototype demonstration in a relevant environment (ground or space).

A major step in the level of fidelity of the technology demonstration follows the completion of TRL 5. At TRL 6, a representative model or prototype system or system - which would go well beyond ad hoc, 'patch-cord' or discrete component level breadboarding - would be tested in a relevant environment. At this level, if the only 'relevant environment' is the environment of space, then the model/prototype must be demonstrated in space.

7. System prototype demonstration in a space environment.

TRL 7 is a significant step beyond TRL 6, requiring an actual system prototype demonstration in a space environment. The prototype should be near or at the scale of the planned operational system and the demonstration must take place in space.

The TRL assessment allows us to consider the readiness and risk of our technology elements, and of the system.

Rad Hard Software

The major problem for Spaceflight computers is

radiation, although there are other environmental issues, and there can always be hardware and software residual errors that made it through testing. This becomes a much bigger problem during long cruise orbits to the outer planets, and for those planets with very large trapped particle fields. The RHS software approach will be flight software running on the Cubesats, and possibly on the main flight computer as well. This section explores approachs to detect and respond to pending radiation damage to flight computers.

This approach is less expensive than flying radiation-hardened CPU's but does come with a risk. The Cubesat rad-hard compute architecture can be developed, but will be a more expensive approach. The software approach needs very thorough testing for validation. Even with Radiation hardened hardware, a "lighter" version of the rad-hard software would be a good approach.

Rad Hard software is an approach that is software-based, and running on the system it is testing. From formal testing results, and with certain key engineering tools, we can come up with likely failure modes, and possible remediation's. Besides self-test, we can have cross-checking of systems. Not everything can be tested by the software, without some additional hardware. First we will discuss the engineering analysis that will help us define the possible hardware and software failure cases, and then we will discuss possible actions and remediations. None is this is new, but the suggestion is to collect together best practices in the software testing area, develop a library of RHS routines, and get operational experience. These routines will be open source.

Another advantage of the software approach is that we can change it after launch, as more is learned, and conditions change.

The RHS has many diverse pieces, and is not just one software module, but can be dispersed. Some of the RHS modules run continuously and some are triggered on demand, due to a specific event. It is desirable to have as much fault/failure coverage as possible, while minimizing the impact on the host's memory and timing.

You're way ahead when you have some idea what is likely to fail, derived from testing, industry reports, and case studies. Fault coverage has to be as complete as possible, but we should ensure we have the known failure modes covered. Of course, some failures were missed in testing, resulting in their presence becoming known even in the operational environment.

It is also critically important to know exactly what software has been loaded into the flight computer. What if you have multiple copies, and don't know which one is in orbit. Configuration Control prevents that, right? It has happened.

There is also now a general policy of "test what you fly, fly what you test." You might have included diagnostic code for integration testing, and pull it out before flight. Wrong. Now the code you are going to fly is untested. The tested version include the instrumentation code. Even though it will never be used, it takes up some space, so cache footprints, memory boundary's, and pipeline contents are different.

We also need to carefully consider the failure recovery. Sometimes, we will need the system to reboot itself. That's disruptive, but necessary in some cases. We want to take every possible path before going down that one.

The flight computers are operating in a hostile environment. There are known failure modes in this environment, that have to be covered. Failures will be transient or hard. Sometimes, hard failures result in a state that is not recoverable. Transient failures, on the other hand, are the hardest to find. We can observe the results, and try to work backward to the root cause. That is where good up-front analysis and data from system test is invaluable. Some architectures, such as the ARM Cortex-R7 have built-in hardware failure detection. That's a good approach, but it leaves many potential failures uncovered.

We can tap industry best practices code for system testing. We can also use testing code developed for system POST (power-on-self-test) as an example. POST is accomplished after a reset, but before the system begins to run operational code. It does allowed for checking internal functionality. POST should certainly be included in our repertoire. POST doesn't have specific run time requirements (except the annoyance threshold). A large block of memory can be tested in sections, to avoid adversely affecting system timing.

Another approach that is catching on is to instantiate a computer architecture (ARM, for example) in a Rad-Hard FPGA.

The Juno Mission

The $1.2 billion ($10^9$) Juno mission to Jupiter arrived after 5 years of travel, and has settled in to making its observations. The spacecraft was launched in August of 2011, and arrived in July 2016. It was placed in Jupiter elliptical polar orbit and was expected to last for 5 years.
It is nowe expected to last until 2025.It was to de-orbit into Jupiter in February 2018. This is to ensure burn-up of the spacecraft to avoid any biological contamination of Jupiter or its moons. It is scheduled to make 37 orbits, but the mission has been extended to July, 2021.The orbit was chosen to minimize contact with Jupiter's intense trapped radiation belts. It's sensitive electronics are housed in "the Juno radiation vault," with 1 cm thick titanium walls. Juno will have available to it some 420 watts of power, from the solar panels, which cover 72 square meters.

The spacecraft weighs over 1,500 kg. It uses 3 solar panels of 2.7 x 8.9 meters long These will be exposed to about 4% of the sunlight at Earth that it would have at Earth. The spacecraft left Florida on an Atlas-V-551 vehicle. The perijove, or closest distance to the planet was planned to be 4,200 km. The highest altitude at apojove is 8.1 million kilometers.

The mission includes infrared and microwave instruments to measure the thermal radiation from

Jupiter's atmosphere, with particularly interest in convection currents. It's data will be used to measure the water in Jupiter's atmosphere, measure atmospheric temperature and composition, and track cloud motions. The mission will also map Jupiter's magnetic and gravity fields. It is expected to probe the magnetosphere in the polar regions and observe the auroras.

Juno uses a bi-propellant propulsion system (for adjustments and insertion manoeuvres) and a monopropellant system for attitude control.

Communications uses X-band to support a data rate of 50 Mbps. The spacecraft will be constrained to 40 Mbytes of camera data per 11-day orbit period.

Large scale Cubesat delivery and support vehicles

In a student project, we used the mission parameters of the Juno mission to Jupiter as far as possible to define the Pinesat mission. The following items and subsystems will be copied from the Juno mission, and are at TRL-9:

Solar panels, power distribution unit, batteries, X-band transceiver and high gain antenna, bi-propellant LEROS1b main engine for trajectory correction, mono-propellant attitude control thrusters.

Atlas-V-551 launch vehicle, TRL-9, seven launches to date, including one to Jupiter.

For the proposed new parts, we assessed the technology, and defined these TRL levels. It has to be taken into account that a TRL derived for an Earth mission might need to be adjusted downward for a long interplanetary cruise, and for operation at Jupiter.

- Inter-cubesat communications – TRL-3.

- Mother ship to cubesat communication – TRL-3.

- Cubesat – TRL-9 for Earth, Moon, and Mars Missions, TRL-7 for Jupiter environment.

- Core Flight System/Core Flight Executive software – TRL-9

- Raspberry Pi flight computer – TRL-9 for Earth missions, TRL-7 for Jupiter environment.

- P-Pod dispenser – TRL-9, TRL-7 for operation at Jupiter, after a long cruise.

- Computer cluster – TRL-7.

- Rad-hard software – TRL-3.

- Onboard EDS relational database – TRL-8.

- Onboard testing of Cubesats before deployment – TRL-9.

- Cubesat Swarm (Cubesat Constellation, 50 units in Earth Orbit, 2015) – TRL-9.

Although Cubesats themselves are at TRL-7, the concept

of cubesat Swarms and Clusters are at TRL levels 3-4.

PineSat

This strawman mission was used as a teaching tool by the author in a Cubesat Engineering and Operations course in the Summer of 2016. The parameters of the Juno Mission to Jupiter were used to bound the problem. We sought to re-implement the mission using Cubesats. This is one possible approach.

The Pinesat vehicle was so named due to its appearance with the cubesat dispensers radiating out from a central core.

The Pinesat mothership design was bounded by the Juno mission parameters of size, weight, power, and communications. Given the specs, we asked the question, how many 1U Cubesats could we accommodate? The answer was one thousand. For operational reasons, we proceeded with 333 3-U Cubesats.

The Pinesat mechanical design is straightforward. The name comes from the fact that the dispenser resembles a pine tree. The Pinesat dispenser has a central hexagonal tube, with the propulsion and electrical power section at the launch vehicle interface end. The avionics and data storage are located in the nose of the vehicle while p-pod's are distributed radially along the central tube. This allows for longitudinal deployment. We postulate having 333 p-pod class dispensers, each with a 3-U cubesat inside.

The Pinesat will keep a database of Electronic Data

Sheets of all the Cubesats. This includes data like state-of-charge, operational status, and instrument complement. This can be updated by a query request from the dispenser's main computer. The Pinesat's main computer will also store its own vehicle's EDS.

The Pinesat dispenser will use the same dual redundant, rad-hard RAD-750 flight computers used on Juno. They have 256 megabytes of flash, 128 megabytes of DRAM, and operate at 200 MHz. They will be running Linux. They will have sufficient storage for the database of the Cubesats' EDS. They will also host an onboard network for communications with the Cubesats when they are onboard, and via radio when they have been deployed. The dispenser vehicle hosts the Swarm's communications links with Earth.

One advantage of the carrier is, like the Shuttle, payloads can be tested before deployment from the carrier. Known bad units can be discarded into Jupiter's atmosphere. The carrier is designed to be modular and adaptable. It is scalable to 100's or 1,000's of Cubesats.

The mothership/dispenser will have a bi-propellant engine for orbit and cruise adjustments, and a monopropellant system for attitude control and reaction wheel momentum unloading.

Cubesats

The Cubesats were 3U format, with identical busses, and varying science instruments. They will have a sun sensor and a magnetic field sensor. Magnetic torquers may be included. They may also include a cold gas propulsion system.

The Cubesats used a Raspberry-Pi flight computer, running NASA/GSFC's CFS/CFE flight software. They will have a sun sensor and a magnetic field sensor. Magnetic torquers may be included. For the payload, different instrumentation will be included on different Cubesats. The Cubesats will be deployed by the mothership as required, to observe and collect data on targets of interest. The Swarm's instrument complement will be defined by the Mission scientists, partially determined by what the Juno mission uncovers.

Ops concept

The Mothership transports the Cubesats to Jupiter unpowered. Every week (tbd), the units are powered on, one at a time, and checked for functionality. The onboard database is updated as required. The results are sent back to the control center on Earth. Most of the mission goals are preplanned and stored in the mothership's computers, but it also will have the flexibility to respond to unanticipated events.

After orbital insertion at Jupiter, and another system check of itself and the Cubesats, the Mothership will deploy a series of Cubesat scouts on a reconnaissance mission, to seek out areas of interest. The Mothership first deploys Cubesats with broad spectral sensing. Based on their findings, the mothership will deploy Cubesats with specific instrumentation to the area of interest. (For example, an advanced thermal imager to an area of

observed thermal activity). The Cubesats are released in the order of necessity. The Cubesats will be able to adjust their attitude with torquer bars to push against the large Jovian magnetic field. We can also include the idea of Cubesat "suicide mission," where the Cubesat plunges into the ring system, or Jupiter's upper atmosphere, and returns data until it is rendered non-functional.
The Cubesats will:

Conduct radio occultation experiments to better categorize the distribution of particles in the rings, by size.

Explore the characteristics of the ring systems, including density, size, distribution, and particle composition. This can also be conducted with synchronized simultaneous observation from multiple observation points.

Explore features visible on on the planetary "surface."

Map the Jovian magnetic field and trapped charged particle environment.

Examine phenomena of opportunity, as they arise.

Be able to respond to targets of opportunity, such as the observed plunge of comet Shumaker-Levy-3 into Jupiter's atmosphere by the Galileo spacecraft.

The Cubesat instruments will be expanded beyond that of Juno. Standard Cubesat busses will support different sensor suites. We have, essentially, 334 observation platforms, including the dispenser. This provides greater mission flexibility.

Cubesat Swarm Exploration of the asteroid belt

As a follow-on to the Pinesat Mission, we expanded and updated the concept, and applied it to exploration of the asteroid belt. Here, the communications and power issues are easier, but the sheer number of targets is overwhelming.

Exploring the asteroids requires a diverse and agile system. A swarm of small spacecraft with different capabilities will be used, combining into Teams to address situations and issues discovered in situ. A intelligent swarm solution to resource exploration of the asteroid belt was proposed by Curtis, et al, in 2003. The concept of Cubesats was not advanced enough at the time for the authors to specifically mention them. They explored issues in local control, networking communications, and implementation in Open Source.
The radiation environment of the asteroid belt is mostly of solar origin, with some Galactic cosmic rays. There is no overall magnetic field to deflect energetic particles. A lot of the material in the belt is dust sized, and will pose a damage threat to spacecraft.

The physical composition of asteroids is varied and poorly understood. The larger Ceres (referred to as a dwarf planet) appears to be composed of a rocky core covered by an icy mantle, and is thought to harbor organic compounds. 4-Vesta may have a nickel-iron core. It was explored by the Dawn spacecraft in 2012. 10-Hygiea appears to have a uniformly primitive composition of carbonaceous chondrite. Many of the smaller asteroids are piles of rubble held together loosely by gravity. Some have moons themselves, or are co-orbiting binary asteroids. The bottom line is, asteroids are diverse. There is even speculation that Ceres may harbor life.

The asteroids are not uniformly distributed. In the asteroid belt, the Kirkwood gaps are relatively empty spots. This is caused by orbital resonance of the asteroids with Jupiter. Orbiting irregularly shaped bodies is challenging, due to the irregular gravity field. This makes station keeping and attitude control a bigger problem.

It has been suggested that asteroids might be used as a source of materials that are rare or exhausted on Earth (asteroid mining) or materials for constructing space habitats and refueling stations for farther missions. Materials that are heavy and expensive to launch from Earth may someday be mined from asteroids and used for in situ space manufacturing. Valuable materials such as platinum and rare and scarce elements may be returned to Earth for a profit.

The Asteroid Swarm, to the greatest extent possible, used the architecture of the Pinesat. There are several major changes. First, the mothership uses a Pi-cluster. The swarm cluster is retained, but the mothership's role is expanded, and has a full control center onboard. This allows it to monitor and respond to individuals quickly. It co-ordinates with and updates the ground based control center. During certain periods, when the mothership is on the opposite side of the Sun from the Earth, it has complete operational control of the Swarm.

Overall Architecture

In this concept, the Cubesats are the primary payload. The Mothership can be thought of as a very large Cubesat. The architecture is kept as close as possible.

Use of a common hardware bus and software architecture for all swarm members, to the greatest extent possible, is a goal. Only the sensor sets will be unique. A Cubesat model for the hardware, and NASA GSFC's Core Flight Software is baselined. A standard linux software operating environment and database will be used.

Each member of the swarm will be aware visually of other swarm members in close proximity. This will be facilitated by having the Mothership as the center of the coordinate system. It will determine its position by celestial navigation. The Cubesats will have a similar capability. The mothership will maintain, as part of its onboard database, the location of all other members. It will also monitor for pending collisions and warn the participants. There will be rules concerning how close swarm members can get to each other, a virtual zone of exclusion. All Earth-based interaction with the swarm will be through the Mothership. Due to varying communication delays, operation of the swarm by teleoperation from Earth is not feasible. The Swarm could be on the opposite side of the Sun from the Earth for extended periods. This is addressed by building autonomy into the system, and a large amount of non-volatile storage will be included for science data.

Use of a common hardware bus and software architecture for all swarm members, to the greatest extent possible, is a goal. Only the sensor sets will be unique. A Cubesat model for the hardware, and NASA GSFC's Core Flight Software is baselined. A standard linux software operating environment and database will be used.

Each swarm member will be equipped with one or more cameras, not only for target investigation, but also for observing the position and relative motions of other swarm members.

Using standard linux clustering software (Beowulf), the Mothership and undeployed swarm members will be able to form an ad-hoc cluster computer to process science data in-situ. Within the Mothership, the use of LAN-based Mesh network was baselined. The Mothership's main computer will be a Raspberry-Pi based cluster.

Batteries and solar panels

The advanced batteries and solar panels on the ongoing Juno mission at Jupiter are functioning well. These would then be a candidate for the Swarm Mothership. Due to technology advances, solar cells can now be used out to 5 AU. The Mothership will have large arrays, but the individual Cubesats have limited area. They will be deployed fully charged. One area of interest is a deployable fabric solar panel.

At the distance of the asteroid belt, the solar constant (kw/meter2) is about ¼ of that at Earth's distance from the sun.

Cubesats

The Cubesats will be a mix of 3U and 6U in size (a U-Unit is 30x10x10 cm), and follow the GSFC-defined PiSat architecture with a Raspberry-Pi flight computer, running NASA/GSFC's CFS/CFE flight software. Different instrumentation will be included on different Cubesats, using common platforms and buses. These will be deployed by the Mothership as required, to observe and collect data on targets of interest. A lander-Cubesat with additional payload and a propulsion system can also be included.

Dispenser/Mothership

The Mothership will be built with standard aerospace products with a mission heritage. We expect to be able to use the same batteries and solar panels from the Juno mission, since the Mothership will be roughly the same size, defined by the size of the launch vehicle shroud. The X-band transceiver on Juno would be a candidate for the Earth link. The carrier is designed to be modular and adaptable. It uses standard PPOD Cubesat deployment mechanisms, oriented radially. Standard p-pod Cubesat dispensers are baselined, but the affects of long term storage of the Cubesats in the dispensers in space must be carefully considered. The effects of cold welding during the transit and storage time needs to be evaluated.

Unlike Earth Cubesat missions, the Cubesats going to the Belt can have their own propulsion. The big limiting factor for them is electrical power. They can't carry large solar arrays. Dispersed from the carrier fully charged, they will operate as long as they can. The electronics and software will be optimized to minimize power usage. More advanced solar arrays, possible fabric-based arrays that will serve double duty as a solar sail, could solve this limitation.

The Mothership provides cloud services to the swarm. It is a store-and-forward node, and the communications relay to Earth. It provides Swarm control, monitoring, and task assignment.

The Mothership will have a bi-propellant engine for orbit and cruise adjustments, and a monopropellant system for attitude control and reaction wheel momentum unloading.

A Swarm exploration of the asteroid belt was proposed by Curtis, et al, in 2003. They baseline about 1,000 units. They define 8-10 types of *Workers,* each with specific capabilities. Units assigned to swarm cohesion and communication they term *Messengers.* There are also Rulers, who function in a managerial role. Cubesats are not specifically mentioned, but the approach is certainly feasible.

A constellation of 50, 2U and 3U Cubesats was deployed in orbit in 2015. Some were released from the ISS, in coordination with a rocket launch. They collected and telemetered data on the lower thermosphere. This was not a swarm per se, but rather 50 units acting on their own, reporting back to their home institutions. Universities around the world participated in the project.

The data came from the region below 85 kilometers, which has enough of an atmosphere to impede spacecraft. The Cubesats collected data as long as they could, as they were reentering the atmosphere. At these altitudes, the rarefied atmosphere can reach temperatures of 2,500 degrees C. It is also a region where the dynamics are controlled by atmospheric tides, themselves controlled by diurnal heating and cooling. The member Cubesats used onboard processing to reduce downlink bandwidth.

Avionics Suite

Both the Mothership and the Cubesats will baseline the GSFC PiSat software and hardware architecture for the flight computers. The Cubesats will use a single unit, and the Mothership will have a 16-unit cluster. Non-deployed Cubesats in the Mothership will be able to participate in the clustering, using the Mothership's internal networking infrastructure. The Mothership will be able to power up and attach selected additional units for particularly computer-intensive tasks.

The Raspberry Pi-3 is a very capable processor. An earlier model was tested to operate to 150 k Rad Total Ionizing Dose, with only the loss of several unused I/O interfaces.   The major source of radiation at the destination will not be trapped particles, but rather ionizing cosmic rays of galactic origin. These are energetic, but sparse. The cluster computer will be enclosed in the nose of the mothership.

A Raspberry Pi-3, requires 3.26 watts of power. It is quad-core, operating at 1.4 GHz. It is a 64-bit machine, with 1 gigabyte of ram, and can achieve 2451 MIPS. It has a dedicated Graphics Processing Unit-based video pipeline that can handle 2D DSP. That is supported by the Open-GL software.

Compute cluster of convenience

Using a variation of the Beowulf clustering software and the communications infrastructure of the Mothership, the Cubesats awaiting deployment can be linked into a Compute cluster configuration. Each compute node will have the Beowulf software pre-loaded as part of its Linux operating system.

Beowulf was developed to provide a low cost solution to linking commodity pc's into a supercomputer. The approach has been applied to clusters of small architectures such as those that serve as flight computers for Cubesats. Several 64-node Pi clusters have been demonstrated in the Earth environment.

The Beowulf cluster is ideal for sorting and classifying data; an example application is the Probabilistic Neural Network. This algorithm has been used to search for patterns in remotely sensed data. It is computationally intensive, but scales well across compute clusters. It was developed by the Adaptive Scientific Data Processing (ASDP) group at NASA/GSFC. The program is available in Java source code.

The first Beowulf cluster to be flown in space was built from twenty 206-MHz StrongARM (SA1110) processors, and flew on the X-Sat, Singapore's first satellite. The performance was 4,000 MIPS. The cluster drew 25 watts. The satellite was a 100 kg unit, 80 CM cube. The cluster was used because the satellite collected large amounts of image data (80 GB per day), most of which was not relevant to the mission. An onboard classification algorithm selected which images would be downloaded. For example, cloudy images were discarded, since land images of Singapore were of interest.

In a cluster, there is always a trade-off of computation and communication, with power draw. This will be monitored and adjusted by the cluster itself.

Surface Lander

In the surface exploration scenario, a 6U Cubesat will serve as a local Mothership. It will be able to detach and deploy the lander vehicle. The orbiting Cubesat can provide a "gods-eye" view, to target locations for direct exploration. It will also serve a a communications relay. The main problem will not be mobility, but rather avoiding floating off the surface.

The ground-based unit will implement prox-ops in a more leisurely fashion, in that motion will be two-dimensional and at low speed. The surface rovers will not be retrieved. The local Mothership may be left at the observation site for additional data, or can be redeployed to an additional target. The location of a lander/rover on the surface will be determined by the orbiting or station-keeping Mothership, with imaging. Standard space communications protocols will be used between the lander and the Mothership, via UHF link.

The Cubesat members will collect observation data on their target, and can conduct radio occultation experiments to better categorize the distribution of particles. They can also conduct synchronized simultaneous observation from multiple observation points of features of interest.

The Mothership is also an observer, with an instrument suite. It can search for magnetic fields, and characterize the charged and energetic particle environment.

Communication methodology within the Cubesat swarm.

ISL (Inter-satelite link) communication will be achieved on Ultra High Frequency (UHF) links. An inter-satellite communication range of 90 Demonstration Satellite (NASA)km to 100km is viable on UHF within the power output range of 4-5 W. The next challenge is regarding selection of the ideal antenna and communication protocol, keeping in mind the existing power and mobility constraints along with the trade-off between radio power and communication distance. NASA's Nodes (Network & Operation Demonstration Satellite) mission, similar in structure to the Edison Demonstration of Smallsat Networks (EDSN) mission, deployed a satellite swarm of Cubesats from the ISS to test inter-satellite communication capabilities in 2015. A primary UHF radio was used for crosslink communication, and a further UHF beacon radio was used for transmitting real time health information of the satellite. In addition to this, position, navigation, and tracking information complement the primary data load. The Cubesats, and the Mothership will use software defined radio, implemented on the flight computer.

Ops concept

During the cruise phase to the Asteroid Belt, the Cubesats are unpowered. Every day or week (tbd), the units are powered on, one at a time, and checked for functionality. The onboard database is updated as required. The results are sent back to the control center on Earth. One advantage of the Mothership is, like the Shuttle, payloads can be tested before deployment Known bad units will be left in place, or discarded into Space.

Near the desired target location at the Asteroid belt, the Mothership uses its main engine to enter solar orbit with the solar panels oriented to the Sun, and the high gain antenna pointed to the Earth.

After another system check of itself and the Cubesats, the Mothership deploys a series of Cubesat scouts on a reconnaissance mission, to seek out areas of interest.

The Mothership deploys Cubesats with broad spectral sensing capabilities. Based on their findings, the Mothership may deploy additional Cubesats with specific instrumentation to the area of interest. (For example, an advanced thermal imager to an area of observed thermal activity). The Cubesats are released in the order of necessity. There will only be one Cubesat per dispenser, so blocking is not an issue.

In the surface exploration scenario, the lander necessarily needs a propulsion system for alignment and touchdown. This would be a cold gas system. It would be possible, but more complex, to implement a sample return. This would involve descent and ascent, return to the Mothership, and rendezvous and docking. It is anticipated that the entire Cubesat with its payload would be returned to Earth, which is simpler than a sample hand-off to a return vehicle.

Fly the Control Center

The Mothership is the navigation reference point for the Cubesats. It obtains its position with respect to Earth from observation, and ground tracking. There will be times when the Earth is not visible form the Mothership's position, so it will use extrapolation and local observation. During these periods of occultation, and also periods of long one-way light times, the Mothership assumes local responsibility for the Health and Safety of the Swarm members. For this, we will implement Control Center functionality within the Mothership. This will take the form of Ball Brother's COSMOS software. This product addresses traditional system test, integration, and flight needs. An additional software module is needed, essentially a virtual Control System Operator. Using defined rules, the Mothership will make decisions concerning the Swarm Members, to the best of its current knowledge. All of this will be documented and downloaded to the Earth-based control center when communications is re-established. An AI capability will be added to Cosmos, in the form of a virtual flight controller agent. Besides the housekeeping functions, we will implement onboard science planning, responsive to on-site conditions, and targets of opportunity.

The Mothership's primary responsibility is continuance of the Mission. To a degree, the Cubesats are considered expendable. During communications black-outs, observations will continue, and the Mothership will dispense explorers according to pre-defined rules, and based on it's best on-scene judgment. It will also continue to collect observation science data, and engineering data related to health and performance across the swarm members.

Wrap-up

They're little, but they're mighty, particularly in groups. The Cubesat architecture lends itself well to groups, especially those which can self-organize and explore. The various technologies for getting the hardware and software together are all available. The concept of flying one large expensive exploration spacecraft may disappear in favor of flying swarms.

References

Balsamo, James M. "CubeSat technology adaptation for in-situ characterization of NEOs," 6th Interplanetary Cubesat Workshop, Cambridge, UK, 30-31 May 2017, avail:
https://icubesat.org/papers/2014-2/2014-b-2-5-cubesat-technology-adaptation-for-in-situ-characterization-of-neos/

Betancourt, Mark "CubeSats to the Moon (Mars and Saturn, too)", Air & Space Magazine, Sept 2014.

Cai, Yaping, et al "Detecting In-Season Crop Nitrogen Stress of Corn for Field Trials Using UAV- and CubeSat-Based Multispectral Sensing, " IEEE J. Selected Topics in Applied Earth Observations and Remote Sensing, issue 12, December 2019.DOI:10.1109/JSTARS.2019.2953489

Challa, Obulapathi N., McNair, Janise "CubeSat Torrent: Torrent-like distributed communications for CubeSat satellite clusters," Military Communications Conference, 2012 , ((MILCOM 2012) July 19, 2016

Challa, Obulapathi N., McNair, Janise "Distributed Data Storage on Cubesat Clusters, Advances in Computing 2013, (3)3 pp.36-49

Challa, Obulapathi N., McNair, Janise "CubeSec and GndSec : a lightweight security solution for Cubesat communications," 26th Annual AIAA/USU Conference on Small Satellites.

Clark, P. E. et al "BEES for ANTS: Space Mission Applications for the Autonomous NanoTechnology Swarm," AIAA, Sept. 2004.avail https://www.researchgate.net/publication/265158396_BE ES_for_ANTS_Space_Mission_Applications_for_the_A utonomous_NanoTechnology_Swarm.

Crusiol, Luis, et all, "Assessing the potential of using high spatial resolution daily NDVI-time-series from planet CubeSat images for crop monitoring," 2021, International Journal of Remote Sensing, V42, Issue 18.

Curtis, S. A. et al "Use of Swarm Intelligence in Spacecraft Constellations for the Resource Exploration of the Asteroid Belt," 2003, Third International Workshop on Satellite Constellations and Formation flying, Pisa, Italy.

Drier, Casey "Cubesats to the moon," Avail: http://www.planetary.org/blogs/casey-dreier/2015/0902-cubesats-to-the-moon.html.

Fortescue, Peter and Stark, John *Spacecraft System Engineering*, 2nd ed, Wiley, 1995, ISBN 0-471-95220-6.

Hall, John "maddog"; Gropp, William *Beowulf Cluster Computing with Linux*, 2003, ISBN -0262692929.

Hinchey, Michael G. ; Rash, James L.; Truszkowski, Walter E.; Rouff, Christopher A., Sterritt, Roy

Autonomous and Autonomic Swarms, avail: https://ntrs.nasa.gov/search.jsp?R=20050210015; 2017-12-20T20:19:24+00:00Z

Jsu, Jeremy "Telescopic Tag Team", Scientific American, Jan 2017, p. 16.

Jones, Nicola "First flight for tiny satellites," Nature, June 2016, Vol 534, p. 15-16.

Kirkpatrick, Brian, et al *Dynamics and Control of Cubesat Orbits for Distributed Space Missions, Aerospace Corporation,* 2015, avail: www.ipam.ucla.edu/wp.../Aerospace-Corp-project-description-FINAL.pdf.

Lappas, Vaios, et al "CubeSail: A low cost Cubesat based solar sail demonstration mission", Advances in Space Research, 2001, 48.11, 1890-1901.

LeMoigne, Jacqueline, et al, "Trade-Space Analysis Tool for Constellations (TAT-C)," NASA/GSFC, avail: https://ntrs.nasa.gov/search.jsp?R=20160014656.

Lewis, H. G. et all, "An assessment of CubeSat collision Risk," 2016, U. Southampton, avail :http://eprints.soton.ac.uk/id/eprint/369583

Ley, w. et all, *Handbook of Space Technology*, AIAA, 2009, ISBN-978-1600867019.

Madni, Mohamed Atef; Raad, Raad; Tubbal, Faisal

"Inter-CubeSat Communications: Routing Between CubeSat Swarms in a DTN Architecture," presentation, avail:.https://icubesat.org/papers/2015-2/2015-b-2-1

Nag, Sreeja, "Design and Evaluation of Distributed Spacecraft Missions for Multi-Angular Earth Observation," April 2015, Dept. of Aeronautics and Astronautics, MIT, PhD. Dissertation.

NASA CubeSat Launch Initiative, *Cubesat 101*, 2017, nasa_csli_cubesat_101_508 .

Pinciroli, Carlo et al "Self-Organizing and Scalable Shape Formation for a Swarm of Pico Satellites" (NASA/ESA Conference on Adaptive Hardware and Systems), 2008, ASIN B00380EAI2.

Pinciroli, Carlo et al "Evolving a Collective Consciousness for a Swarm of Pico-Satellites," avail: http://carlo.pinciroli.net/publications.php

Robson, Christopher, "Comparison of CubeSats, Cubesat Swarms and Classical Earth Observation Satellites in LEO, Canadian SmallSat Conference, 2016.

Ruggueri, Marina et al "The Flower constellation set and its Possible Applications, Final Report," avail: www.esa.int/act

Safyan, Mike "Overview of the Planet Labs Constellation of Earth Imaging Satellites," March 2015, presentation, avail: https://www.itu.int/en/ITU-

R/space/workshops/2015...sat/.../Planet-Labs-Safyan.pdf

Santilli, Giancarlo; Vendittozzi, Cristian; Cappellett, Chantal; Battistin; Simone; Gessini, Paolo, *CubeSat constellations for disaster management in remote areas,* 2017, Acta Astronautica, April 2018, Pages 11-17, Volume 145.
https://www.sciencedirect.com/science/article/abs/pii/S00 94576517303168

Staehle, Robert et al, "Interplanetary Cubesats: Opening the Solar System to a Broad Community at Lower Cost," Cubesat Workshop 2011 Logan Utah.

Stakem, Patrick H.; Martinez, José Carlos; Chandrasenan, Vishnu; Mittras, Yash; "A Cubesat Swarm Approach for the Asteroid Belt," Presented to NASA Goddard Planetary CubeSats Symposium, August 16-17, 2018, NASA, GSFC, Greenbelt, MD.

Ticker, R. L. ,Azzolini, J. D. *2000 Survey of Distributed Spacecraft Technologies and Architectures for NASA's Earth Science Enterprise in the 2010-2025 Timeframe,* April 2000, NASA/TM-2000-209964.

Tonn, Shara, "How swarms of small satellites could revolutionize space exploration," Oct. 2016, Stanford Engineering, avail: https://engineering.stanford.edu/news/

Truszkowski, Walt, et al *Autonomous and Autonomic Systems: With Applications to NASA Intelligent*

Spacecraft Operations and Exploration Systems, Springer, 1st Edition 2009, ISBN-1846282322.

Truszkowski, Walt; Clark, P. E.;, Curtis, S.; Rilee, M. Marr, G. "ANTS: Exploring the Solar System with an Autonomous Nanotechnology Swarm," J. Lunar and Planetary Science XXXIII (2002).

Truszkowski, Walt "Prototype Fault Isolation Expert System for Spacecraft Control," N87-29136, avail: https://ntrs.nasa.gov/search.jsp?R=19870019703,

Van der Ha, Jozef C. (ed) *"Mission Design & Implementation of Satellite Constellations"* Proceedings of an International Workshop, held in Toulouse, France, Conference Proceedings, Springer, November 1997, ISBN-978-9401061377.

Virgili, Bastide et al "Mega-constellations Issues," 41st COSPAR Scientific assembly, 2016, avail:http://cospar2016.tubitak.gov.tr/en/

Wertz, James R. (ed) *Spacecraft Attitude Determination and Control*, 1980, Kluwer, ISBN 90-277-1204-2.

Wood, Dr. Lloyd "Introduction to Satellite constellations, orbital types, uses and related facts," Presentation, ISU summer session, July 2006, avail: savi.sourceforge.net/about/lloyd-wood-isu-summer-06-constellations-talk.pdf

Wua, Shufan, et all *"A multiple-CubeSat*

constellation for integrated earth observation and marine/air traffic monitoring," 2021, in Advances in Space Research, Vol. 67, No. 11. https://www.sciencedirect.com/science/article/abs/pii/S02 73117720302635

Wikipedia, various.

Resources

nasa.gov/smallsat-instutite/cubesats-gsfc

Small Spacecraft Technology State of the Art, NASA-Ames, NASA/TP2014-216648/REV1, July 2014.

Core Flight System (CFS) Deployment Guide, Ver. 2.8, 9/30/2010, NASA/GSFC 582-2008-012.

Cubesat Design Specification, Cubesat Program, California Polytechnic State University, avail:
https://www.google.com/search?
q=Cubesat+Design+Specification&ie=utf-8&oe=utf-8
and at www.Cubesat.org

Cubesat Concept and the Provision of Deployer Services, avail:
https://eoportal.org/web/eoportal/satellite-missions/content/-/article/Cubesat-concept-1

NASA systems Engineering Handbook, NASA SP-2007-6105.   Avail:
https://ntrs.nasa.gov/archive/nasa/casi.ntrs.nasa.gov/2008
0008301.pdf

www.ccsds.org

https://nasasearch.nasa.gov/

Here is a 3-D model of a Cubesat that you can download, print on heavy cardstock, and assemble.

http://www.space.aau.dk/Cubesat/kits.html

Spacetrack.org (requires an account)

http://www.celestrak.com/NORAD/elements/

http://satellitedebris.net/Database/

NASA, Software Documentation Standard, NASA-STD-2100-91,
available:https://ntrs.nasa.gov/archive/nasa/casi.ntrs.nasa.gov/19980228459.pdf

"MakerSat: A Cubesat Designed for In-Space 3D Print and Assembly," SSC16-WK-29,
avail: digitalcommons.usu.edu/cgi/viewcontent.cgi?article=3444&context=smallsat

NASA, John F. Kennedy Space Center, Launch Services Program, Program Level Dispenser and Cubesat Requirements Document, LSP-REQ-317.01, Rev. B, Jan. 2014.

FCC, Guidance on Obtaining Licenses for Small Satellites, March 15, 2013, 13-445. avail: https://www.fcc.gov/document/guidance-obtaining-licenses-small-satellites

Amateur Radio Satellite Organization (AMSAT) – www.amsat.org

General Payload Users Guide, Spaceflight, Inc. SF-2100-

PUG-00001, www.spaceflightindustries.com, NASA Open Source Agreement, avail: https://opensource.org/licenses/NASA-1.3

InterPlanetary Networking Special Interest Group (IPNSIG) - http://ipnsig.org/

"CubeSat: A new Generation of Picosatellite for Education and Industry Low-Cost Space Experimentation," avail: users.csc.calpoly.edu/~csturner/ssc01.pdf

Rapid Build and Space Qualification of Cubesats, avail: www.digitalcommons.usu.edu/cgi/viewcontent.cgi?article=1148&context=smallsat

Open Source Engineering Tools

http://wiki.developspace.net/Open_Source_Engineering_Tools
AVM Dynamics Satellite Constellation Modeler, https://www.avmdynamics.com/index1.htm

SaVi Satellite Constellation Visualization, http://savi.sourceforge.net/

100 Earth Shattering Remote Sensing Applications and Uses, 2015, GIS Geography avail: http://gisgeography.com/100-earth-remote-sensing-applications-uses/

Report Concerning Space Data Systems Standards,

Mission Operations Services Concept, CCSDS Informational Report, CCSDS 520.0-G-3, Green Book, December 2010, avail, ccsds.org

Overview of Space Communications Protocols, Avail: cwe.ccsds.org/sls/docs/SLS.../130x0g2_master_Dec16_2 013.docx

Core Flight System – http://cfs.gsfc.nasa.gov

https://cubesatcookbook.com

http://pmddtc.state.gov/

http://srag-nt.jsc.nasa.gov/SpaceRadiation/What/What.cfm

http://www.jpl.nasa.gov/cubesat/missions/

http://www.computescotland.com/future-spacecraft-clusters-5240.php

http://www.astrome.co/blogs/the-art-of-satellite-constellation-design-what-you-need-to-know/

Kicksat Nanosatellite Mission, https://directory.eoportal.org/web/eoportal/satellite-missions/k/kicksat http://carlo.pinciroli.net/publications.php

https://satellitesafety.gsfc.nasa.gov/

NASA's Mission Operations and Communication Services (pricing), Oct.. 2014, avail:https://deepspace.jpl.nasa.gov/files/dsn/NASA_MO&CS.pdf

Wikipedia, various.

Glossary

1553 – Military standard data bus, serial, 1 Mbps.

1U – one unit for a Cubesat, 10 x 10 x 10 cm.

3U – three units for a Cubesat

6U – 6 units in size, where 1u is defined by dimensions and weight.

802.11 – a radio frequency wireless data communications standard.

AACS – (JPL) Attitude and articulation control system.

ACE – attitude control electronics

Actuator – device which converts a control signal to a mechanical action.

Ada – a computer language.

A/D, ADC – analog to digital converter

AFB – Air Force Base.

AGC – Automated guidance and control.

AIAA – American Institute of Aeronautics and Astronautics.

AIST – NASA GSFC Advanced Information System Technology .

ALU – arithmetic logic unit.

AmSat – Amateur Satellite. Favored by Ham Radio operators as communication relays.

Analog – concerned with continuous values.

ANSI – American National Standards Institute

ANTS – Autonomous NanoTechnology Swarm.

Android – an operating system based on Gnu-Linux, popular for smart phones and tablet computers.

Antares – Space launch vehicle, compatible with Cubesats, by Orbital/ATK (U.S.)

AP – application programs.

API – application program interface; specification for software   modules to communicate.

APL – Applied Physics Laboratory, of the Johns Hopkins University.

Apm – antenna pointing mechanism

Apollo – US manned lunar program.

Arduino – a small, inexpensive microcontroller architecture.

Arinc – Aeronautical Radio, Inc. commercial company supporting   transportation, and providing standards for avionics.

ARM – Acorn RISC machine; a 32-bit architecture with wide application in embedded systems.

ARPA – (U. S.) Advanced Research Projects Agency.

ArpaNet – Advanced Research Projects Agency (U.S.), first packet switched network, 1968.

ASIC – application specific integrated circuit

Async – non synchronized

ATAC – Applied Technologies Advanced Computer.

ATP – authority to proceed

AU – astronomical unit. Roughly 93 million miles, the mean distance between Earth and Sun,

BAE – British Aerospace.

Baud – symbol rate; may or may not be the same as bit rate.

BCD – binary coded decimal. 4-bit entity used to represent 10 different decimal digits; with 6 spare states.

Beowolf – a cluster of commodity computers; multi-processor, using Linux.

Big-endian – data format with the most significant bit or

byte at the lowest address, or transmitted first.

Binary – using base 2 arithmetic for number representation.

BIST – built-in self test.

Bit – binary variable, value of 1 or 0.

Boolean – a data type with two values; an operation on these data types; named after George Boole, mid-19th century inventor of Boolean algebra.

Bootloader – initial program run after power-on or reset. Gets the computer up & going.

Bootstrap – a startup or reset process that proceeds without external intervention.

BSD – Berkeley Software Distribution version of the Bell Labs Unix operating system.

BP - bundle protocol, for dealing with errors and disconnects.

BSP – board support package. Customization Software and device drivers.

Buffer – a temporary holding location for data.

Bug – an error in a program or device.

Bus – an electrical connection between 2 or more units; the engineering part of the spacecraft.

Byte – a collection of 8 bits

C – programming language from Bell Labs, circa 1972.

cache – temporary storage between cpu and main memory.

Cache coherency – process to keep the contents of multiple caches consistent,

CalPoly – California Polytechnic State University,. San Luis Obispo, CA.

CAN - controller area network bus.

CCSDS – Consultive Committee on Space Data Systems.

CDR – critical design review
C&DH – Command and Data Handling
CDFP CCSDS File Delivery Protocol
cFE – Core Flight Executive – NASA GSFC reusable
    flight software.
CFS – Core Flight System – NASA GSFC reusable
    flight software.
Chip – integrated circuit component.
Clock – periodic timing signal to control and synchronize
    operations.
CME – Coronal Mass Ejection. Solar storm.
CMOS – complementary metal oxide semiconductor; a
    technology using both positive and negative
    semiconductors to achieve low power operation.
CogE – cognizant engineer for a particular discipline;
    go-to guy;   specialist.
Complement – in binary logic, the opposite state.
Compilation – software process to translate source code
    to assembly or machine code (or error codes).
Configware – equivalent of software for FPGA
    architectures; configuration information.
Constellation – a grouping of satellites.
Control Flow – computer architecture involving directed
    flow through the program; data dependent paths
    are allowed.
COP – computer operating properly.
Coprocessor – another processor to supplement the
    operations of the main processor. Used for floating
    point, video, etc.   Usually relies on the main
    processor for instruction fetch; and control.
Cordic – Coordinate Rotation Digital Computer – to
    calculate hyberbolic and trig functions.

Cots – commercial, off the shelf

CPU – central processing unit

CRC – cyclic redundancy code – error detection and correction mechanism.

Cubesat – small inexpensive satellite for colleges, high schools, and individuals.

D/A – digital to analog conversion.

DAC – digital to analog converter.

Daemon – in multitasking, a program that runs in the background.

DARPA – Defense advanced research projects agency.

Dataflow – computer architecture where a changing value forces recalculation of dependent values.

Datagram – message on a packet switched network; the delivery, arrival time, and order of arrival are not guaranteed.

dc – direct current.

D-cache – data cache.

DDR – dual data rate memory.

Deadlock – a situation in which two or more competing actions are each waiting for the other to finish, and thus neither ever does.

DCE – data communications equipment; interface to the network.

Deadly embrace – a deadlock situation in which 2 processes are each waiting for the other to finish.

Denorm – in floating point representation, a non-zero number with a magnitude less than the smallest normal number.

Device driver – specific software to interface a peripheral to the operating system.

Digital – using discrete values for representation of states or numbers.

Dirty bit – used to signal that the contents of a cache have changed.

Discrete – single bit signal.

DMA – direct memory access.

Dnepr – Russian space launch system compatible with Cubesats.

DOD – (U. S.) Department of Defense.

DOE – (U. S.) Department of Energy.

DOF – degrees of freedom.

Downlink – from space to earth.

Dram – dynamic random access memory.

DSP – digital signal processing/processor.

DTE – data terminal equipment; communicates with the DCE to   get to the network.

DTN – delay tolerant networks.

DUT – device under test.

ECC – error correcting code

EDAC – error detecting and correction circuitry.

EDAC – error detection and correction.

EGSE – electrical ground support equipment

EIA – Electronics Industry Association.

ELV – expendable launch vehicle.

Embedded system – a computer systems with limited human interfaces and performing specific tasks. sually part of a larger system.

EMC – electromagnetic compatibility.

EMI – electromagnetic interference.

EOL – end of life.

EOS – Earth Observation spacecraft.

Ephemeris – orbital position data.

Epitaxial – in semiconductors, have a crystalline

overlayer with a well-defined orientation.

EPS – electrical power subsystem.

ESA – European Space Organization.

ESRO – European Space Research Organization

ESTO – NASA/GSFC – Earth Science Technology Office.

Ethernet – networking protocol, IEEE 802.3

ev – electron volt, unit of energy

EVA – extra-vehicular activity.

Exception – interrupt due to internal events, such as overflow.

EXPRESS racks – on the ISS, EXpedite the PRocessing of Experiments for Space Station Racks

FAA – (U S.) Federal Aviation Administration.

Fail-safe – a system designed to do no harm in the event of failure.

Falcon – launch vehicle from SpaceX.

FCC – (U.S.) Federal Communications Commission.

FDC – fault detection and correction.

Firewire – IEEE-1394 standard for serial communication.

Firmware – code contained in a non-volatile memory.

Fixed point – computer numeric format with a fixed number of digits or bits, and a fixed radix point.

Flag – a binary state variable.

Flash – non-volatile memory

Flatsat – prototyping and test setup, laid out on a bench for easy access.

FlightLinux – NASA Research Program for Open Source code in space.

Floating point – computer numeric format for real numbers; has significant digits and an exponent.

FPGA – field programmable gate array.

FPU – floating point unit, an ALU for floating point numbers.

Full duplex – communication in both directions simultaneously.

Fram – ferromagnetic RAM; a non-volatile memory technology

FRR – Flight Readiness Review

FSW – flight software.

FTP – file transfer protocol

Gbyte – 109 bytes.

GEO – geosynchronous orbit.

GeV – billion (109) electron volts.

GNC – guidance, navigation, and control.

Gnu – recursive acronym, gnu is not unix.

GPIO – general purpose I/O.

GPL – gnu public license used for free software; referred to as the "copyleft."

GPS – Global Positioning system – Navigation satellites.

GPU – graphics processing unit. ALU for graphics data.

GSFC – Goddard Space Flight Center, Greenbelt, MD.

Gyro – (gyroscope) a sensor to measure rotation.

Half-duplex – communications in two directions, but not simultaneously.

HAL/S – computer language.

Handshake – co-ordination mechanism.

HDL – hardware description language

Hertz – cycles per second.

Hexadecimal – base 16 number representation.

Hi-rel – high reliability

HPCC – High Performance Computing and Communications.

Hypervisor – virtual machine manager. Can manage

multiple operating systems.

I2C – a serial communications protocol.

IARU – International Amateur Radio Union

I-cache – Instruction cache.

ICD – interface control document.

IC&DH – Instrument Command & Data Handling.

IEEE – Institute of Electrical and Electronic engineers

IEEE-754 – standard for floating point representation and calculation.

IIC – inter-integrated circuit (I/O).

IMU – inertial measurement unit.

Integer – the natural numbers, zero, and the negatives of the natural numbers.

Interrupt – an asynchronous event to signal a need for attention (example: the phone rings).

Interrupt vector – entry in a table pointing to an interrupt service routine; indexed by interrupt number.

IP – intellectual property; Internet protocol.

IP core – IP describing a chip design that can be licensed to be used in an FPGA or ASIC.

IP-in-Space – Internet Protocol in Space.

IR – infrared, 1-400 terahertz. Perceived as heat.

IRAD – Independent Research & Development.

ISA – instruction set architecture, the software description of the computer.

ISO – International Standards Organization.

ISR – interrupt service routine, a subroutine that handles a particular interrupt event.

ISS – International Space Station

I&T – integration & test

ITAR – International Trafficking in Arms Regulations (US Dept. of State)

ITU – International Telecommunications Union

IV&V – Independent validation and verification.

JEM – Japanese Experiment Module, on the ISS.

JHU – Johns Hopkins University.

JPL – Jet Propulsion Laboratory

JSC – Johnson Space Center, Houston, Texas.

JTAG – Joint Test Action Group; industry group that lead to IEEE 1149.1, Standard Test Access Port and Boundary-Scan Architecture.

JWST – James Webb Space Telescope – follow on to Hubble.

Kbps – kilo (103) bits per second.

Kernel – main portion of the operating system. Interface between the applications and the hardware.

Kg – kilogram.

kHz – kilo (10^3) hertz

KVA – kilo volts amps – a measure of electrical power

Ku band – 12-18 Ghz radio

Lan – local area network, wired or wireless

LaRC – (NASA) Langley Research Center.

Latchup – condition in which a semiconductor device is stuck in one state.

Lbf – pounds-force.

LEO – low Earth orbit.

Let- Linear Energy Transfer

Lidar – optical radar.

Linux – open source operating system.

List – a data structure.

Little-endian – data format with the least significant bit or byte at the highest address, or transmitted last.

Logic operation – generally, negate, AND, OR, XOR, and their inverses.

Loop-unrolling – optimization of a loop for speed at the cost of space.

LRR – launch readiness review

LRU – least recently used; an algorithm for item replacement in a cache.

LSB – least significant bit or byte.

LSP – (NASA) launch services program, or launch services provider

LUT – look up table.

MANET - mobile ad-hoc network.

Master-helped – control process with one element in charge. Master status may be exchanged among elements.

Mbps – mega (10^6) bits per second.

Mbyte – one million (10^6 or 2^{20}) bytes.

Memory leak – when a program uses memory resources but does not return them, leading to a lack of valuable resources.

Memory scrubbing – detecting and correcting bit errors.

MEMS – Micro Electronic Mechanical System.

MESI – modified, exclusive, shared, invalid state of a cache coherency protocol.

MEV – million electron volts.

MHz – one million (106) Hertz

Microcontroller – monolithic cpu + memory + I/O.

Microkernel – operating system which is not monolithic, functions execute in user space.

Microprocessor – monolithic cpu.

Microsat – satellite with a mass between 10 and 100 kg.

Microsecond – 10-6 second.

Microkernel – operating system which is not monolithic; functions execute in user space.

MLI – multi-layer insulation.

MPA – multiple payload adapter for deploying multiple - pod's

MPE – Maximum predicted environments.

mram – magnetorestrictive random access memory.

mSec – Millisecond; (10-3) second.

MIPS – millions of instructions per second.

MMU – memory management unit; manned maneuvering unit.

MSB – most significant bit or byte.

Multiplex – combining signals on a communication channel by   sampling.

Multicore – multiple processing cores on one substrate or chip; need not be identical.

Mutex – a software mechanism to provide mutual e exclusion between tasks.

Nano – 10^{-9}

NanoRacks – a company providing a facility onboard the ISS to support Cubesats.

nanoSat – small satellite with a mass between 1 and 10 kg.

NASA - National Aeronautics and Space Administration.

NDA – non-disclosure agreement; legal agreement protecting IP.

NEO – Near Earth object.

NEN – (NASA's) Near Earth Network

Nibble – 4 bits, ½ byte.

NIST – National Institute of Standards and Technology (US), previously, National Bureau of Standards.

NMI – non-maskable interrupt; cannot be ignored by the software.

Normalized number – in the proper format for floating

point representation.

NRCSD - NanoRack CubeSat Deployer

NRE – non-recurring engineering; one-time costs for a project.

NSF – (U.S.) National Science Foundation.

NSR – non-space rated.

NTIA (U.S.) National Telecommunications an

NUMA – non-uniform memory access for multiprocessors; local and global memory access protocol.

NVM – non-volatile memory.

NWS – (U.S.) National Weather Service

Nyquist rate – in communications, the minimum sampling rate, equal to twice the highest frequency of the signal.

OBC – on board computer

OBD – On-Board diagnostics.

OBP – On Board Processor

Off-the-shelf – commercially available; not custom.

OpAmp – (Linear) operational amplifier; linear gain and isolation stage.

OpCode – encoded computer instruction.

Open source – methodology for hardware or software development distribution and access.

Operating system – software that controls the allocation of resources in a computer.

OSAL – operating system abstraction layer.

OSI – Open systems interconnect model for networking, from ISO.

Overflow - the result of an arithmetic operation exceeds the capacity of the destination.

Packet – a small container; a block of data on a network.

Paging – memory management technique using fixed size memory blocks.

Paradigm – a pattern or model

Paradigm shift – a change from one paradigm to another. Disruptive or evolutionary.

Parallel – multiple operations or communication proceeding simultaneously.

Parity – an error detecting mechanism involving an extra check bit in the word.

Pc – personal computer.

PC-104 – standard for a board (90 x 96 mm), and a bus for embedded use.

PCB – printed circuit board.

pci – personal computer interface (bus).

PCM – pulse code modulation.

PDR – preliminary design review

Peta - 10^{15} or 2^{50}

Phonesat – small satellite using a cell phone for onboard control and computation.

Picosat – small satellite with a mass between 0.1 and 1 kg.

Piezo – production of electricity by mechanical stress.

Pinout – mapping of signals to I/O pins of a device.

Pipeline – operations in serial, assembly-line fashion.

PiSat – a Cubesat architecture developed at NASA-GSFC, base on the Raspberry Pi architecture.

Pixel – picture element; smallest addressable element on a display or a sensor.

PLL – phase locked loop.

PocketQube – smaller than a Cubesat; 5 cm cubed, a mass of no more than 180 grams, and uses COTS components.

Poc – point of contact

POSIX – IEEE standard operating system.

PPF – payload processing facility

PPL – preferred parts list (NASA).

P-POD – Cubesat launch dispenser, Poly-Picosatellite Orbital Deployer

Psia – pounds per square inch, absolute.

PWM – pulse width modulation.

Python – programming language.

Quadrature encoder – an incremental rotary encoder providing rotational position information.

Queue – first in, first out data buffer structure; implemented in hardware or software.

Rad – unit of radiation exposure

Rad750 – A radiation hardened IBM PowerPC cpu.

Radix point – separates integer and fractional parts of a real number.

RAID – redundant array of inexpensive disks.

Ram – random access memory.

RBF – remove before flight.

Real-time – system that responds to events in a predictable, bounded time.

Register – temporary storage location for a data item.

Reset – signal and process that returns the hardware to a known, defined state.

RF – radio frequency

RFC – request for comment

RHPPC – Rad-Hard Power PC.

RISC – reduced instruction set computer.

Router – networking component for packets.

RS-232/422/423 – asynchronous and synchronous serial communication standards.

RT – remote terminal.

RTC – real time clock.

RTOS – real time operating system.

SAM – sequential access memory, like a magnetic tape.

Sandbox – an isolated and controlled environment to run untested or potentially malicious code.

SDR – software defined radio

SDRAM – synchronous dynamic random access memory.

Segmentation – dividing a network or memory into sections.

Semiconductor – material with electrical characteristics between conductors and insulators; basis of current technology processor, memory, and I/O devices, as well as sensors.

Semaphore – a binary signaling element among processes.

SD – secure digital (non-volatile memory card).

SDVF – Software Development and Validation Facility.

Sensor – a device that converts a physical observable quantity or event to a signal.

Serial – bit by bit.

SEU – single event upset (radiation induced error).

Servo – a control device with feedback.

SIMD – single instruction, multiple data (parallel processing)

Six-pack – a six U Cubesat, 10 x 20 x 30 cm.

SMP – symmetric multiprocessing.

Snoop – monitor packets in a network, or data in a cache.

SN – (NASA's) Space Network

SOA – safe operating area; also, state of the art.

SOC – system on a chip; also state-of-charge.

Socket – an end-point in communication across a network

Soft core – a hardware description language description of a cpu core.

Software – set of instructions and data to tell a computer what to do.

SMP – symmetric multiprocessing.

Snoop – monitor packets in a network, or data in a cache.

Spacewire – high speed (160 Mbps) link.

SPI - Serial Peripheral Interface - a synchronous serial communication interface.

SRAM – static random access memory.

Stack – first in, last out data structure. Can be hardware or software.

Stack pointer – a reference pointer to the top of the stack.

STAR – self test and repair.

State machine – model of sequential processes.

STOL – system test oriented language, a scripting language for testing systems.

T&I – test and integration.

Terrabyte – 10^{12} bytes.

SAA – South Atlantic anomaly. High radiation zone.

SEB – single event burnout.

SEU – single event upset.

SEL – single event latchup.

SoC – state of charge; system on a chip.

Soft core – hardware description description language model of a logic core.

spi – serial peripheral interface

SpaceCube – an advanced FPGA-based flight computer.

SpaceWire – networking and interconnect standard.

Space-X – commercial space company.

SRAM – static random access memory.

Stack – first in, last out data structure. Can be hardware or software.

Stack pointer – a reference pointer to the top of the stack.

State machine – model of sequential processes.

Strawman – a simple first draft, or prototype, to be improved later.

SWD – serial wire debug.

Synchronous – using the same clock to coordinate operations.

System – a collection of interacting elements and relationships with a specific behavior.

System of Systems – a complex collection of systems with pooled resources.

Suitsat – old Russian spacesuit, instrumented with an 8-bit micro, and launched from the ISS.

Swarm – a collection of satellites that can operate cooperatively.

sync – synchronize, synchronized.

TCP/IP – Transmission Control Protocol/Internet protocol.

TDRSS – Tracking and Data Relay satellite system.

Tera - 10^{12} or 2^{40}

Test-and-set – coordination mechanism for multiple processes that allows reading to a location and writing it in a non-interruptible manner.

TCP/IP – transmission control protocol/internet protocol; layered set of protocols for networks.

Thread – smallest independent set of instructions managed by a multiprocessing operating system.

TID – total ionizing dose.

TMR – triple modular redundancy.

Toolchain – set of software tools for development.

Transceiver – receiver and transmitter in one box.

Transducer – a device that converts one form of energy to another.

Train – a series of satellites in the same or similar orbits, providing sequential observations.

TRAP – exception or fault handling mechanism in a computer; an operating system component.

Triplicate – using three copies (of hardware, software, messaging, power supplies, etc.). for redundancy and error control.

TRL – technology readiness level

Truncate – discard. cutoff, make shorter.

TT&C – tracking, telemetry, and command.

ttl – transistor-transistor logic integrated circuit.

UART – Universal asynchronous receiver-transmitter.

UDP – User datagram protocol; part of the Internet Protocol.

uM – micro (10^{-6}) meter

Underflow – the result of an arithmetic operation is smaller than the smallest representable number.

UoSat – a family of small spacecraft from Surrey Space Technology Ltd. (UK).

uplink – from ground to space.

USAF – United States Air Force.

USB – universal serial bus.

VDC – volts, direct current.

Vector – single dimensional array of values.

VHDL – very high level design language.

VIA – vertical conducting pathway through an insulating layer.

Virtual memory – memory management technique using

address translation.

Virtualization – creating a virtual resource from available physical resources.

Virus – malignant computer program.

Viterbi Decoder – a maximum likelihood decoder for data encoded with a Convolutional code for error control. Can be implemented in software or hardware.

VLIW – very long instruction word – mechanism for parallelism.

VxWorks – real time operating system from Wind River systems.

WiFi – short range digital radio.

Watchdog – hardware/software function to sanity check the hardware, software, and process; applies corrective action if a fault is detected; fail-safe mechanism.

Wiki – the Hawaiian word for "quick." Refers to a collaborative content website.

Word – a collection of bits of any size; does not have to be a power of two.

Write-back – cache organization where the data is not written to main memory until the cache location is needed for re-use.

Write-through – all cache writes also go to main memory.

X-band – 7 – 11 GHz.

Xilinx – manufacturer of programmable logic and FPGA's.

Zener – voltage reference diode.

Zero address – architecture using implicit addressing, like a stack.

Zombie-sat – a dead satellite, in orbit.

Zone of Exclusion – volume in which the presence of an object or personnel, or activities are prohibited.

If you enjoyed this book, you might also enjoy one of my other books.

16-bit Microprocessors, History and Architecture, 2013 PRRB Publishing, ISBN-1520210922.

4- and 8-bit Microprocessors, Architecture and History, 2013, PRRB Publishing, ISBN-152021572X,

Apollo's Computers, 2014, PRRB Publishing, ISBN-1520215800.

The Architecture and Applications of the ARM Microprocessors, 2013, PRRB Publishing, ISBN-1520215843.

Earth Rovers: for Exploration and Environmental Monitoring, 2014, PRRB Publishing, ISBN-152021586X.

Embedded Computer Systems, Volume 1, Introduction and Architecture, 2013, PRRB Publishing, ISBN-1520215959.

The History of Spacecraft Computers from the V-2 to the Space Station, 2013, PRRB Publishing, ISBN-1520216181.

Floating Point Computation, 2013, PRRB Publishing, ISBN-152021619X.

Architecture of Massively Parallel Microprocessor Systems, 2011, PRRB Publishing, ISBN-1520250061.

Multicore Computer Architecture, 2014, PRRB Publishing, ISBN-1520241372.

Personal Robots, 2014, PRRB Publishing, ISBN-1520216254.

RISC Microprocessors, History and Overview, 2013, PRRB Publishing, ISBN-1520216289.

*Robots and Telerobots in Space Application*s, 2011, PRRB Publishing, ISBN-1520210361.

The Saturn Rocket and the Pegasus Missions, 1965, 2013, PRRB Publishing, ISBN-1520209916.

Visiting the NASA Centers, and Locations of Historic Rockets & Spacecraft, 2017, PRRB Publishing, ISBN-1549651205.

Microprocessors in Space, 2011, PRRB Publishing, ISBN-1520216343.

Computer *Virtualization and the Cloud*, 2013, PRRB Publishing, ISBN-152021636X.

What's the Worst That Could Happen? Bad Assumptions, Ignorance, Failures and Screw-ups in Engineering Projects, 2014, PRRB Publishing, ISBN-1520207166.

Computer Architecture & Programming of the Intel x86 Family, 2013, PRRB Publishing, ISBN-1520263724.

The Hardware and Software Architecture of the Transputer, 2011,PRRB Publishing, ISBN-152020681X.

Mainframes, Computing on Big Iron, 2015, PRRB Publishing, ISBN- 1520216459.

Spacecraft Control Centers, 2015, PRRB Publishing, ISBN-1520200617.

Embedded in Space, 2015, PRRB Publishing, ISBN-1520215916.

A Practitioner's Guide to RISC Microprocessor Architecture, Wiley-Interscience, 1996, ISBN-0471130184.

Cubesat Engineering, PRRB Publishing, 2017, ISBN-1520754019.

Cubesat Operations, PRRB Publishing, 2017, ISBN-152076717X.

Interplanetary Cubesats, PRRB Publishing, 2017, ISBN-1520766173 .

Cubesat Constellations, Clusters, and Swarms, Stakem, PRRB Publishing, 2017, ISBN-1520767544.

Graphics Processing Units, an overview, 2017, PRRB

Publishing, ISBN-1520879695.

Intel Embedded and the Arduino-101, 2017, PRRB
Publishing, ISBN-1520879296.

Orbital Debris, the problem and the mitigation, 2018,
PRRB Publishing, ISBN-*1980466483.*

Manufacturing in Space, 2018, PRRB Publishing, ISBN-
1977076041.

NASA's Ships and Planes, 2018, PRRB Publishing,
ISBN-1977076823.

Space Tourism, 2018, PRRB Publishing, ISBN-
1977073506.

STEM – Data Storage and Communications, 2018,
PRRB Publishing, ISBN-1977073115.

In-Space Robotic Repair and Servicing, 2018, PRRB
Publishing, ISBN-1980478236.

*Introducing Weather in the pre-K to 12 Curricula, A
Resource Guide for Educators,* 2017, PRRB Publishing,
ISBN-1980638241.

*Introducing Astronomy in the pre-K to 12 Curricula, A
Resource Guide for Educators,* 2017, PRRB Publishing,
ISBN-198104065X.
Also available in a Brazilian Portuguese edition, ISBN-
1983106127.

Deep Space Gateways, the Moon and Beyond, 2017, PRRB Publishing, ISBN-1973465701.

Exploration of the Gas Giants, Space Missions to Jupiter, Saturn, Uranus, and Neptune, PRRB Publishing, 2018, ISBN-9781717814500.

Crewed Spacecraft, 2017, PRRB Publishing, ISBN-1549992406.

Rocketplanes to Space, 2017, PRRB Publishing, ISBN-1549992589.

Crewed Space Stations, 2017, PRRB Publishing, ISBN-1549992228.

Enviro-bots for STEM: Using Robotics in the pre-K to 12 Curricula, A Resource Guide for Educators, 2017, PRRB Publishing, ISBN-1549656619.

STEM-Sat, Using Cubesats in the pre-K to 12 Curricula, A Resource Guide for Educators, 2017, ISBN-1549656376.

Embedded GPU's, 2018, PRRB Publishing, ISBN-1980476497.

Mobile Cloud Robotics, 2018, PRRB Publishing, ISBN-1980488088.

Extreme Environment Embedded Systems, 2017, PRRB

Publishing, ISBN-1520215967.

What's the Worst, Volume-2, 2018, ISBN-1981005579.

Spaceports, 2018, ISBN-1981022287.

Space Launch Vehicles, 2018, ISBN-1983071773.

Mars, 2018, ISBN-1983116902.

X-86, 40th Anniversary ed, 2018, ISBN-1983189405.

Lunar Orbital Platform-Gateway, 2018, PRRB Publishing, ISBN-1980498628.

Space Weather, 2018, ISBN-1723904023.

STEM-Engineering Process, 2017, ISBN-1983196517.

Space Telescopes, 2018, PRRB Publishing, ISBN-1728728568.

Exoplanets, 2018, PRRB Publishing, ISBN-9781731385055.

Planetary Defense, 2018, PRRB Publishing, ISBN-9781731001207.

Exploration of the Asteroid Belt, 2018, PRRB Publishing, ISBN-1731049846.

Terraforming, 2018, PRRB Publishing, ISBN-

1790308100.

Martian Railroad, 2019, PRRB Publishing, ISBN-1794488243.

Exoplanets, 2019, PRRB Publishing, ISBN-1731385056.

Exploiting the Moon, 2019, PRRB Publishing, ISBN-1091057850.

RISC-V, an Open Source Solution for Space Flight Computers, 2019, PRRB Publishing, ISBN-1796434388.

Arm in Space, 2019, PRRB Publishing, ISBN-9781099789137.

Search for *Extraterrestrial Life,* 2019, PRRB Publishing, ISBN-978-1072072188.

Submarine Launched Ballistic Missiles, 2019, ISBN-978-1088954904.

Space Command, Military in Space, 2019, PRRB Publishing, ISBN-978-1693005398.

Robotic Exploration of the Icy moons of the Gas Giants, ISBN- 979-8621431006.

History & Future of Cubesats, ISBN-978-1986536356.

Robotic Exploration of the Icy Moons of the Ice Giants, by Swarms of Cubesats, ISBN-979-8621431006.

Swarm Robotics, ISBN-979-8534505948.

Introduction to Electric Power Systems, ISBN-979-8519208727.

Powerships, Powerbarges, Floating Wind Farms: electricity when and where you need it, 2021, PRRB Publishing, ISBN-979-8716199477.

Centros de Control: Operaciones en Satélites del Estándar CubeSat (Spanish Edition), 2021, ISBN-979-8510113068.

The Artemis Missions, Return to the Moon, and on to Mars, 2021, ISBN-979-8490532361.

James Webb Space Telescope. A New Era in Astronomy, 2021, ISBN-979-8773857969.